DARDANELLES
A Midshipman's Diary, 1915-16

H. M. Denham

DARDANELLES

Published by Sapere Books.
20 Windermere Drive, Leeds, England, LS17 7UZ,
United Kingdom

saperebooks.com

Copyright © The Estate of H.M. Denham, 1981.
First published by John Murray (Publishers) Ltd, 1981.
The Estate of H.M. Denham has asserted its right to be identified as the author of this work.
All rights reserved.

No part of this publication may be reproduced, stored in any retrieval system, or transmitted, in any form, or by any means, electronic, mechanical, photocopying, recording, or otherwise, without the prior written permission of the publishers.

ISBN: 978-1-80055-067-4.

TABLE OF CONTENTS

PREFACE 7
PROLOGUE: JOINING *AGAMEMNON* 8
ONE: VOYAGE TO THE DARDANELLES 16
TWO: BOMBARDMENT OF THE OUTER FORTS 20
THREE: LANDING OF DEMOLITION PARTIES 41
FOUR: PRELIMINARY BOMBARDMENT OF NARROWS' FORTS 51
FIVE: MINESWEEPING — OUR INADEQUATE EQUIPMENT 57
SIX: FLEET'S FINAL ATTACK ON THE NARROWS 63
SEVEN: PREPARATIONS FOR LANDING MILITARY EXPEDITION 70
EIGHT: LANDINGS ON GALLIPOLI 93
NINE: *AGAMEMNON* REFITS AT MALTA 124
TEN: MILITARY FRUSTRATION ON GALLIPOLI 132
ELEVEN: NEW LANDINGS AT SUVLA BAY 145
TWELVE: TRANSPORT LOSSES AND FRUSTRATION 168
THIRTEEN: ARRIVAL OF LORD KITCHENER 176
FOURTEEN: WINTER STORMS AND HEAVY CASUALTIES 178
FIFTEEN: EVACUATION OF GALLIPOLI 183
A REFLECTION ON THE DARDANELLES CAMPAIGN 198
SIXTEEN: GOOD-BYE TO *AGGIE* 200
AFTERMATH 202
A NOTE TO THE READER 205

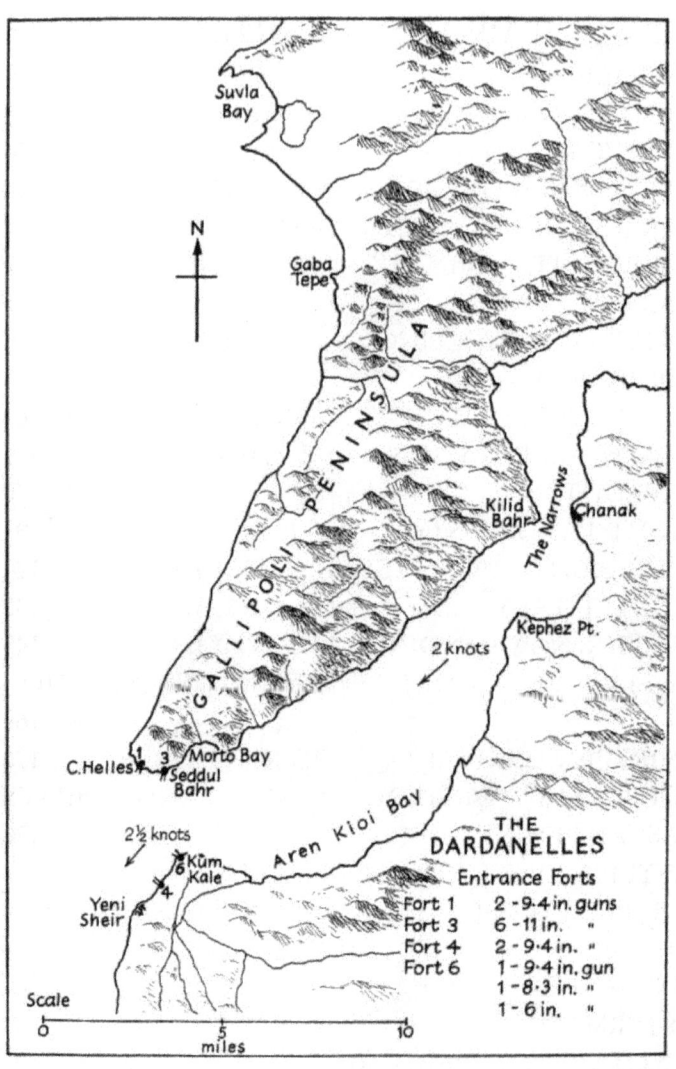

PREFACE

There comes a time when one decides upon disposing of one's collection of old documents, reports and diaries. I was recently busy with the destruction of First World War diaries when a friend of mine, Simon Young, intervened and asked to see anything I might have not yet destroyed. I made a summary of the remaining copies concerning mostly my antics at the Dardanelles in 1915-16, but this summary was not good enough and I was asked for an exact copy of the original diaries. All italic sections are my additional comments on the diary to help give the reader some further information.

My first volume of the diary having already been destroyed, I have written a summary of earlier events leading up to the surviving diary when I went to the Dardanelles.

I am grateful to Miss Zillah Pettitt for the improvement in my line drawings done at the time of making notes for the diary; to Mr Michael Crookshank, son of our popular Lt Crookshank, for his help with his father's records; to Dr Ronald Hope (Marine Society); to Mr George Millar; to Mr John Paton (Commonwealth War Graves Commission); to Lt-Comdr W. Ratcliffe; to Rear-Admiral Dalrymple Smith for refreshing my memory on gunnery problems; and to Rear-Admiral Dunbar-Nasmith for helping me to check his father's records.

H.M.D.

PROLOGUE: JOINING *AGAMEMNON*

August 1914 saw me in my last term at the Royal Naval College, Dartmouth. All that term there had been a sense of foreboding: we knew that war with Germany lay close ahead. On Saturday, August 1st, at 4 p.m. came the Admiralty telegram 'Mobilise'. We were spread all over the playing fields and the news was greeted by us 420 cadets with a resounding cheer: at last we were to fight the Germans. We ran to our college dormitories to pack our sea-chests ready for transport to various warships. There was no confusion as we already knew our ships and where to join them. Soon the market carts, already alerted in the countryside, began to arrive and were carrying our chests down to Dartmouth and across to the waiting trains at Kingswear Station.

It was all tremendously exciting for us young cadets and, as my train steamed along the river bank of the Dart on its way to Devonport, I felt a nostalgia for those happy sailing days in the Black Cutters and Montague whalers. Soon we were passing the old three-decker *Britannia*, whose decks I had often explored, and I remembered the occasion when I had climbed up the rigging and for a bet reached the truck of the fore topgallant mast.

I was one of the 'sixteen-year-olds' who, following Mr Gieve's advice in his booklet *How to Become a Naval Officer*, had been made to take the plunge at twelve and a half and to don naval uniform for our two years' training at Osborne Naval College and a further two at Dartmouth. Our years at Dartmouth had been much the happier and as the months passed we had realised that a war with Germany was surely in the offing and had frequently discussed, with some relish, the part we might have to play.

I had been appointed to one of the last of the Victorian battleships, *Exmouth*, reported to be lying at Devonport; but when we reached Devonport, *Exmouth* was not to be found in port and we were accommodated in the barracks where we discussed the impending war. It was generally believed that war could not last longer than three weeks and our fear was that we might miss the chance of fighting.

TUESDAY, AUGUST 4TH. At 11 p.m. Great Britain declared war on Germany and early the following morning we left Devonport by train for Portland hoping to find *Exmouth*. Arriving that afternoon we reported to the dockyard, only to find that *Exmouth* had sailed that very morning. However, *Agamemnon*'s picket-boat came alongside and took us on board; this ship turned out to be our war appointment. We were 12 cadets, and already there were four midshipmen and six sub-lieutenants — altogether 22 in our mess in the gunroom. (This was a reasonably spacious compartment, with two scuttles (portholes) permitting daylight where we ate, worked, read and wrote our letters. We slept in our hammocks in the adjoining chest flat.)

Having deluded ourselves into thinking we had attained some level of importance as the senior cadets at Dartmouth we now came down to earth with a tremendous bump. This strange contrast in our daily life afloat began by tumbling out of our hammocks at 5.30 a.m. to double bare-footed round the upper deck.

We were chased around all day learning something of our duties, action stations and boat work. All the while we were made to feel we were the scum of the earth, known to the sub-lieutenants as the 'warts'.

A certain amount of mild bullying in the form of 'evolutions' took place in the gunroom occasionally at dinner during our early weeks on board. This was very unpleasant. 'Evolutions' will be well remembered by my contemporaries at sea during this period. Such terms as 'Breadcrumbs', 'Dogs of War', 'Fork in the Beam' and 'Angostura Trail' will come to mind. Evolutions were devised so that the unfortunate 'warts' could be beaten hard on the backside with a dirk-scabbard by the senior sub-lieutenant. This traditional form of bullying had died out before the end of the War.

When off duty we spent most of our time between decks either in the gunroom or the adjoining chest flat. In our sea-chests were all our clothes and belongings just as they had been during our four years at Osborne and Dartmouth. It was therefore most annoying and discomforting for us when we learnt quite suddenly that Admiralty, on account of fire risks, had ordered all midshipmen's chests to be landed. Messrs Gieve, outfitters of almost every naval officer, undertook to store the chests for the duration of the War and to replace them with tin cases which, of course, were most inconvenient. Our pay remained at 1s/9d per day, but Admiralty paid us also 1s as messing allowance.

Agamemnon, generally known to the sailors as *Aggie*, was the last of the old 'broadside' battleships and though laid down in 1903 before the revolutionary centre-line turret *Dreadnought*, she was actually in service after her, having taken three years until she could be commissioned. A 12-in. armour belt gave her excellent protection, but her speed was only 18 knots. She was the last heavy ship to have reciprocating engines.

From early August until December 31st *Agamemnon*, together with the rest of the Channel fleet, patrolled the Channel to 'cover the passage of the Expeditionary Force to France'. To cover against what? No one could explain. There was no sign of the enemy until New Year's Day 1915 when our first tragedy of war at sea gave us a nasty jolt.

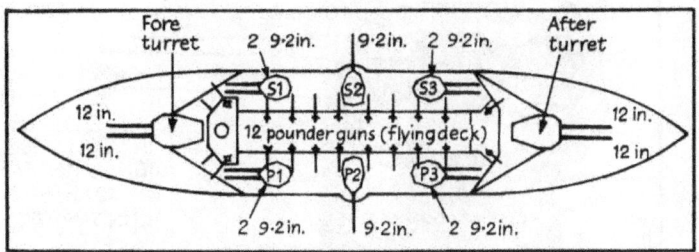

Agamemnon: main and secondary armament

On *Friday January 1st 1915*, during the early hours of a dark rough night, the fleet was off Lyme Bay steaming at 10 knots on a westerly course. I was called at a quarter to midnight to keep the Middle Watch and I remember tumbling out of my hammock to find the ship rolling about so much that I was nearly seasick. At 2.15 our next astern — the old battleship *Formidable* — suddenly hauled out of the line to port and the cruiser *Diamond* on the flank turned with her. There was no signal and, I remember at the time, no cause for alarm. Meanwhile the wind was increasing to gale force 9 and the barometer fell to 28.8 in. At 3.20 rockets were seen, apparently from *Formidable*. Twenty minutes passed. Then the Admiral signalled 'Raise steam for 17 knots' and soon the fleet was heading for Portland, entering harbour at 8.15 a.m. At 11.15 a.m. *Topaze* came into harbour with her fore topgallant mast blown away and with 43 survivors of *Formidable* on board. This was our first authentic news of the disaster.

At 2.15 p.m. *Diamond* could be seen approaching, and, like *Topaze*, without her topgallant masts. She was signalling on her Morse-lamp the names of survivors she had aboard — 22 men and 14 officers, including one of my best friends, Midshipman Eustace Guinness, a very strong swimmer.

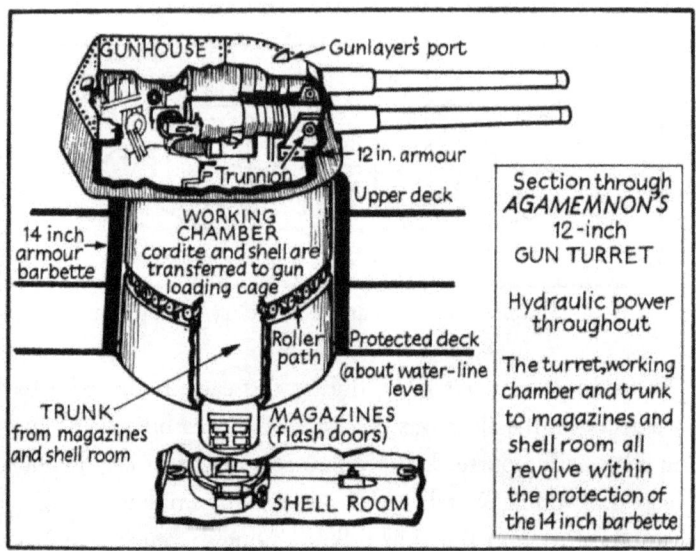

Section through Agamemnon's 12-in. gun turret. Hydraulic power throughout. The turret, working chamber and trunk to magazines and shellroom all revolved within the protection of the 14-in. barbette

We soon learned that *Formidable* had sunk after having been torpedoed twice. She was struck first at 2.20 a.m. on the starboard bow forward and, owing to the heavy sea, started to list to starboard badly by the bows. This caused her lights to go out and the main steam pipe to burst. She stopped and was in darkness for a long time before capsizing and sinking. The two cruisers, *Diamond* and *Topaze*, were able to save many lives because they could lie broadside-on to the gale and the consequent huge seas close to leeward of the sinking *Formidable*. Hence, providing the survivors could remain afloat, they were soon swept down by the waves to the rescuing cruisers which had trailed ropes or nets over the side. As long as they could hold on, in their weakened state, the survivors were soon hauled aboard and revived with warm clothing and hot cocoa.

In mid-January, quite unexpectedly, *Agamemnon*, together with the rest of the Channel Fleet, went to Quiberon Bay to practise gunnery for two weeks, sometimes firing at sea targets and sometimes at shore targets. We were never told the reason for the shore targets, but the subject of the Dardanelles had often been discussed among ourselves.

In early November 1914 Britain had declared war on Turkey and soon after our two battle-cruisers, *Indefatigable* and *Indomitable*, for some obscure reason, had been ordered to have a preliminary bang at the outer forts of the Dardanelles. Later we heard rumours of a War Cabinet decision to attack the Dardanelles. Was this what it was all about?

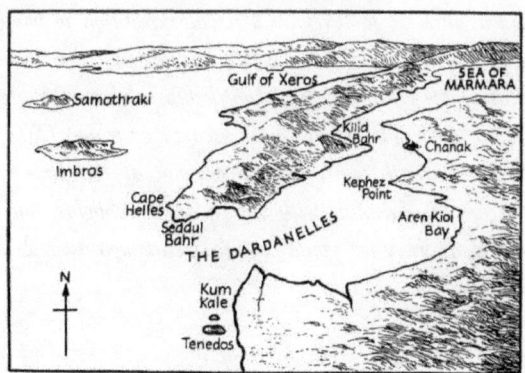

A bird's-eye view of the Dardanelles

The Ottoman Empire entered the war on the German side in October 1914, and our War Cabinet's first discussion on how to attack Turkey took place in London late in November. Here Winston Churchill, as First Lord of the Admiralty, supported by Admiral Lord Fisher (First Sea Lord), proposed a joint naval-military attack on Gallipoli as the best method, not only of defending Egypt, but of controlling the Dardanelles passage. (At this time 12,000 ships a year used to pass through.)

Since troops were not available the proposed plan was shelved until January 2nd 1915 when our Ambassador at St Petersburg telegraphed to London that Grand Duke Nicholas, as head of the Russian armies, asked for Britain to provide some form of help to relieve the severe pressure by Turkish troops on the Russian army in the Caucasus.

It was Lord Kitchener, who decided that our help must be the forcing of the Dardanelles, but since troops were still not available it must be a naval operation with the object of cutting the Turkish Empire in two, supplying Russia with munitions, and at the same time securing our defence of Egypt.

Churchill pleaded in vain for troops, Admiral Fisher threatened to resign. Admiral Carden, in the Mediterranean, sent an unenthusiastic reply on the possibilities of success; but nevertheless by the end of January Admiralty was directed to 'Prepare a naval expedition to bombard and take the Gallipoli peninsula with Constantinople as its objective'.

We had available a number of old battleships and some cruisers due to be scrapped anyhow. They were to be used to overcome 150 somewhat outdated heavy Turkish guns, but we did not at this time give much thought to a means of dealing with minefields, searchlights, and howitzer batteries, especially when we would have to operate against a 2- to 3-knot current gushing out of the Dardanelles.[1]

---

[1] All italic sections are author's comments after the war had ended.

My action station at this time was the after 12-in. turret, commanded by a Lt Studd stationed in the gunhouse, together with a midshipman (myself) and 16 seamen. We manned the two guns, loading and laying them, as well as training the turret and working the rangefinder. The expert hydraulic engineer had the rating of Armourer and ranked as a Chief Petty Officer. He really knew his stuff.

The laying of the guns and the training of the turret were directed by instruments from the fore-top, but in the event of control being shot away we could maintain the gunfire ourselves — 'local control'.

Below the gunhouse in the working chamber were four seamen and another armourer, and below that came the magazines, handling-room, and shell room, each with a Petty Officer and eight men (10 in shell room).

Thus, 50 of us would sometimes be shut up in these very confined spaces for many hours on end, and you can imagine our joy at the end of a long stuffy day when the order was passed to 'secure' and we could disperse to more spacious quarters.

ONE: VOYAGE TO THE DARDANELLES

Back at Portland early in February, 48 hours' leave was granted suddenly to each watch, and we knew that something was afoot. No sooner were we back than *Agamemnon* received orders to raise steam for full speed. Despite our 57 leave-breakers, partially replaced by men from other ships, we weighed anchor and put to sea under sealed orders at 9 p.m. on Tuesday February 9th.

Full of anticipation that we might be off to fight our most recent enemy, the Turks, we were soon steaming down channel, and two days later passing the Burlings and later approaching Gibraltar Strait. Still none of us knew exactly where we were making for except the Captain who later announced that we were to join the Flag of Admiral Carden at Malta. We had naturally begun to think more about the Dardanelles, and the next day Fluter gave a lecture to all officers on proposed operations to be adopted should we have to bombard the Dardanelles. We now understood that it could be a naval attack to force the passage through the Straits to Constantinople, and, consequently, we were thrilled at the prospect of this exciting adventure at last.

I must explain here that Fluter was the rather impolite name we had imposed upon Captain Fyler, our fearless leader, lacking any sense of humour and having a flair for pronouncing many words in a most peculiar manner; to him anyone of eastern Europe was an Aborigine — pronounced 'Aborojine'. Cap Grisnez was always 'Grisnis' and we midshipmen were always the 'young gentlemen'. Later, to vent our feelings on Guest Nights, we sang songs with verses composed of his latest sayings which we were always listening for or indeed provoking. 'The Rabbit' was our Commander, C. St Claire Cameron, who, being of a milder nature was constantly bullied by Fluter. Some of us sometimes went so far as provoking one against the other in order to record a new verse for our next song on the coming Guest Night!

On *Monday February 15th* soon after 4 p.m. we entered Malta Grand Harbour: we passed close to merchant steamers and some of H.M. ships. There were several steamers of the Clan line ('turret ships') and other merchant ships putting to sea.

H.M. ships in here were *Prince George* (temporary flag of Admiral Carden), *Canopus, Albion, Majestic, Irresistible, Courbet*, and *Jean Bart*, which was in dry dock having her bows repaired after being struck by an Austrian torpedo; *Dartmouth, Sapphire, Blenheim* and submarine *B 11* (Lieutenant Holbrook) refitting. French ships *Democratie, Waldeck, Rousseau, Foudre* (aeroplane carrier), *Diderot, Protet* (T.B.D.), a smaller destroyer and a submarine. According to intelligence officers, we heard that Admiralty is prepared to sacrifice four to six ships over the Dardanelles operation, so it seemed like serious business at last.

As soon as we had berthed in harbour, a signal was received from flagship: 'Rig a crow's-nest fitted with telephonic communication, as high up as possible for spotting corrections'. Little did I realise that this was to be my action station for much of the coming operations!

We had previously asked for 1,500 tons of coal and 500 tons of oil fuel. Coaling was arranged by shore labour and soon 16 lighters of coal were brought alongside and the task of taking it in began.

Shore labour, which was also available at Alexandria and Port Said, involved a large number of local men. Each carried a half-hundredweight basket of coal (usually poised on the left shoulder) up the inclined planks from the lighters alongside to the ship's upper deck and then tipped the coal down into the bunker chutes. So many men were employed in this endless stream that 'coaling ship' went quickly.

Almost all ships still burnt coal, and in my diary there is mention of coaling Agamemnon *from a collier almost every week. This involved all the ship's company, officers and men. It might be thought a disagreeable task, but it was not unpleasant and we took to it with enthusiasm. It was highly competitive among the four 'parts of ship', i.e. fo'c'sle, foretop, maintop and quarterdeck, on the basis of 'tons per hour'. We shovelled the coal in the collier's hold into 2-cwt bags, a number of these (six to ten) were stropped together, then winched up to the derrick heads and swung onto the upper deck of* Agamemnon *to be carried off by trollies and tipped into the ship's bunkers. A careful tally was kept on each of the four holds by an officer, otherwise we all worked side by side — officers and men. I always tried to get the job of working the winch, especially if it had a 'swinging derrick' — requiring much more skill, and it was fun.*

We all got very black but as we distilled our own fresh water — nearly 20 tons a day — there was no trouble in cleaning ourselves afterwards.

TUESDAY FEBRUARY 16TH. Coaling continued all night and was not completed until 8.30 a.m. After this, we were washing down and then embarking oil fuel, stores and ammunition; also some coils of wire rope, which we were to embark for delivery to the new battleship *Queen Elizabeth*, expected to arrive shortly.

War has not upset the more peaceful life of the Maltese, who were all dressed up enjoying their annual carnival.

WEDNESDAY FEBRUARY 17TH. At 6.20 we were 15 miles

due south of Malta, when we sighted *Queen Elizabeth* steaming E. She looked a fine new ship, with her eight 15-in. guns, but with her present engine-trouble can steam only 14 knots instead of 25. We stopped engines and transferred by sea-boat our coils of wire. Then, *Agamemnon*, being senior officer, ordered *Queen Elizabeth* to take station astern while we steamed in line-ahead formation at 14 knots for the Kithera Channel and, eventually, the Dardanelles.

THURSDAY FEBRUARY 18TH. During the forenoon we went to Gen. Quarters and at the same time *Queen Elizabeth* opened fire on our target with her heavy guns and also her 6-in. guns. She probably fired full charge and with her 'director fire' (the very modern way of laying and directing the fire of all the main armament from the control tower) she did remarkably well, getting 'straddles' nearly every time.

'Full charge firing' implied that four ¼-charges of cordite were used for the purpose of getting long range and deep penetration, but it wore out the rifling of the gun. 'Straddling' a target meant that some shots were over and others short.

During the 1st Dog Watch we sighted the island of Antikithera (at the entrance to the Aegean) and passing through that passage at 6.26 p.m. we altered course to N.E. by E. into the Aegean. We had a hockey game during the 1st Dog but a wave came over the quarterdeck and spoilt it for us. We are shoving along at 15 knots now and are due to arrive Tenedos or Lemnos at 4 p.m. tomorrow; we hope to go into action tomorrow afternoon.

FRIDAY FEBRUARY 19TH. At 6.50 a.m. we were passing through the Doro Channel and expect to arrive at the Dardanelles this afternoon.

TWO: BOMBARDMENT OF THE OUTER FORTS

All around the Entrance were scattered the various bombarding ships *Inflexible* (flag Vice-Admiral Carden), *Albion*, *Cornwallis*, *Triumph*, *Vengeance*, and the French battleships *Bouvet*, *Suffren*, *Charlemagne*, also the cruiser *Dublin*, some of our destroyers and two French submersibles which were spotting for the firing being carried out slowly and at long range, about 12,000 yds. We saw the aircraft-carrier *Ark Royal* at Tenedos with aeroplanes, one of which was about to ascend. Also at anchor were *Irresistible*, colliers and destroyers. We passed Rabbit Island which is small and uninhabited, and as we drew near *Inflexible* we stopped engines and everyone watched the bombardment being about 17,000 yds from the forts and out of their range. After Quarters and physical drill everyone came on deck again to see the bombardment, which was a fine sight to watch.

Cornwallis was engaging the forts of Seddul Bahr at about 10,000 yds; *Bouvet* and *Vengeance* engaged the Kum Kale forts. At 4.30 p.m. *Cornwallis*, closing to about 7,000 yds, got no reply to her fire. Two of our aeroplanes were up over Rabbit Island. Five minutes later *Bouvet*, supporting *Cornwallis*, opened fire on Seddul Bahr forts. Forts on both sides were now getting covered with dust and earthworks demolished by bursting shells — Fort No. 6 seemed to be knocked out; but at 4.52 forts on both sides again fired, especially No. 4. *Cornwallis* and *Vengeance* immediately replied and increased range, firing effectively with 6-in. guns as well as 12-in. Just before this incident General Recall was hoisted but as soon as the forts were found still active, it was immediately negatived. Number 6 Fort fired very close to *Vengeance*, and *Bouvet* opened fired against Seddul Bahr forts. A Turkish destroyer now appeared near the mouth of the Dardanelles but made off at full speed when fired on by *Bouvet*.

At 5.00 p.m. received the much-longed-for signal: '*Agamemnon* support *Cornwallis*.' With a terrific cheer 'Action' was sounded off, cutters were topped back and within two or three minutes a lot of the unnecessary gear was cleared away from upper deck such as uprights, wood, etc. and turrets were closed up, but we were prepared to go into action wearing ordinary clothes, aft deck scuttles open, nothing flooded and not even the stanchions down. Forts now firing vigorously all round *Vengeance* and *Cornwallis*. 5.05 p.m. *Bouvet* getting fired on heavily. We are closing in at 10 knots to help *Cornwallis*. *Suffren* and *Charlemagne* also coming up to assist and open fire at about 9,000 yds. Action now general. At 5.13 we opened fire with P1 turret and fired each 9.2 in turn, one gun at a time; we started at 10,000 yds and closing to just over 7,000, which was very close, and they were blazing away at us, some falling very near but most of them were well over. At 5.20 P1 fired on the village but we ceased fire temporarily, as we were now getting too close, so we turned 16 points still firing.

In the after turret we got off only one round, but that was a beauty, bursting right on one of their turrets at the fort. Altogether about a dozen rounds were fired, three being direct hits, the others mostly over; all our shells burst kicking up a lot of dust. The Turks fired seven or eight shells at us but none hit; one passed between the masts, another 100 yds astern, others mostly over. (They were 8-in. or 9-in.)

We now ceased firing and all ships steamed out from the forts towards Tenedos in line-ahead formation at about 8 knots proceeding seawards.

Our two aeroplanes which had been observing over the forts now returned to the *Ark Royal* at Tenedos and signalled: 'As far as can be seen guns in No. 1 Fort are both intact, two also in No. 4; three are in place in No. 3 on South Face. The gun crews were seen running back to their guns at No. 1 Fort when *Vengeance* closed in and it appears necessary that buildings adjacent Fort S also require shelling as the enemy evidently remained in them during early part of bombardment.'

SATURDAY FEBRUARY 20TH. Squadron joined up at daylight and proceeded to Tenedos Island, but soon it came on to blow so the whole Allied fleet weighed and proceeded for shelter to the other side of the island and anchored there. In the forenoon we cleared for immediate action; all bedding, tin cases, wood, gear, etc. was down below, fighting lights were lit and everyone wearing Fighting Whites (those which I have had ready for six months now!). It was really grand fun, almost as good as the action we were in yesterday and everyone enjoyed it thoroughly. In the gunroom we even threw overboard a large number of books; but, alas, eventually bad weather prevented our going into action today and so much to everyone's disgust we replaced gear.

During the afternoon a destroyer went right into the coast to estimate the damage we did yesterday, and though she went within range of the forts the latter did not attempt to molest her. W/T signal from *Ark Royal*: 'Owing to strong winds aeroplanes will be unable to ascend, unless wind moderates.' But it did not, hence no bombardment.

It is reported that the six German submarines being transported by rail to the Dardanelles were all pilfered of their machinery while passing through Romania and so are rendered useless.

W/T signal from Ark *Royal*: 'Two seaplanes flying over forts yesterday between 4.30 p.m. and 5.20 p.m. report that guns in No. 1 Fort are uninjured. During heavy bombardment (4.30 to 5.30 p.m.) of Fort 3 most shots fell over and to the left. Damage to Forts 3 and 6 could not be observed owing to smoke. Convinced excellent results obtained by arbitrary spotting. Request trial.'

Aircraft were still a novelty. We remembered several occasions, some five years ago in 1910 when we were cadets at Osborne, a naval Lieutenant, Samson, trying to fly one of our earliest seaplanes on the Medina River. Now we discovered that he had become a Commander with 18 aircraft based at Tenedos. I had access to some of his signals to Admiralty pleading that only five of his aeroplanes were fit for action and asking for four Farman 100 h.p. planes to help replace casualties.

There was also our first aircraft-carrier, Ark Royal, *an ugly converted steamer with a launching ramp built over the bows. She seemed to carry a motley collection of aircraft: I found on board her a big Wright machine capable of 105 m.p.h., some seaplanes, a couple of Short two-seaters, and two Sopwiths which, owing to their low h.p., were sometimes, especially in a calm, unable to rise from the sea.*

Also, for the purpose of spotting for battleship bombardments there was the captive kite-balloon housed in the converted merchant-ship Hector. *We sometimes saw the balloon being shot at and having to be hauled down in a hurry.*

Many times in my diary I find such entries as 'air reconnaissance not possible', 'unable to understand your spotting corrections', 'cannot locate battery'. As far as Agamemnon *was concerned, we achieved little benefit from air spotting, although air reconnaissance was generally very helpful.*

The Germans also operated a few seaplanes but the occasional bomb did not cause us much inconvenience.

Now we received the Admiral's first Operation Order: Operation Order No. 1. Phase 1. Feb. 20th 1915 *Inflexible*.

I. The reduction of the forts at entrance to Dardanelles will be continued on Feb. 21st.

II. General Plan: *Vengeance, Cornwallis, Suffren* and *Charlemagne* working in pairs will run in to 3,000 yds and engage Forts Nos. 1 and 4 with their secondary armaments, aiming to destroy each individual gun by a direct hit.

Admiralty had informed us the Outer Forts were armed as follows:

No. 1: Two 24-cm guns
No. 2: Six field-guns
No. 3: Six 28-cm guns
No. 4: Two 24-cm guns
No. 5: Five field-guns
No. 6: Facing N.W. — one 28-cm, one 26-cm, one 24-cm; Facing N. — two 28-cm, one 26-cm, one 24-cm; Facing N.E. — one 15-cm, one 21-cm.

III. In support: *Agamemnon, Queen Elizabeth, Irresistible* and *Gaulois* firing at long range and deliberately on Forts 1, 3, 4 & 6 respectively with the object of preventing the defenders manning their guns.

IV. (a) Ships of each pair are to be at such a distance apart that the one can support the other while turning.

(b) Each run will commence by order of the V.A. Commanding.

(c) 2nd ship of a pair must not turn in the wake of the leader.

V. (a) Supporting ships will anchor in positions indicated and range on forts.

(b) The action having commenced, supporting ships will open a slow fire on their forts by order of flagship.

(c) *Agamemnon* and *Queen Elizabeth* will use threequarter charges from 9.2-in. to 15-in. guns.

(d) *Agamemnon* and *Inflexible* are to check fire while their forts are being closely engaged by the inshore ships.

Signed
Vice-Admiral Carden

Extract from Admiralty Orders for Reduction of Dardanelles Defences: To be carried out in seven phases:

1. Reduction of defences at entrance to Straits in Bashika Bay, and on north coast of Gallipoli.
2. Sweeping minefields at entrance and reducing defences up to and not further than the Narrows.
3. Reduction of forts at Narrows.
4. Sweeping of principal minefields.
5. Silencing of forts above Narrows.
6. Passage of fleet through Dardanelles.
7. Operations in Sea of Marmara and establishing patrol in Dardanelles. Each ship is to have an observation party under a capable officer. Their duties are as follows:

(a) Locate and immediately report position of enemy's defence.

(b) Time each battery etc. as it opens fire.

(c) Observe enemy's fire and result of our firing.

((b) and (c) should be signalled as quickly as possible.)

For observing enemy's fire, ships must not only report on that experienced by themselves but also on fire directed on other ships. The fall of shot relative to target, range and bearings on which enemy's guns fire must be noted. Directly a gun battery has been located accurately it is to be placed on the numbered square map made out. By signalling these positions, ships may be kept fully informed of all defences. *Irresistible* and *Albion* both have howitzers mounted on their turrets, which are to deal with field guns mounted in villages along the Straits. Two destroyers in Phase 2 are detailed to destroy torpedo tubes set in the banks of the Straits. There are two tubes known to be at Seddul Bahr and Kum Kale as well as many others. A good lookout to be kept for floating mines, and ships must keep out of main stream as much as possible.

During the preliminary bombardment each ship is to send out a picket-boat to steam on the 'off' quarter of the ship ready to throw a net over a mine or destroy it by rifle-fire. When nets are used, each boat is to tow the mine away before sinking it; each boat to carry several nets.

The fleet under Vice-Admiral Carden's command is:

1st Division:
Inflexible (flag)
Agamemnon
Queen Elizabeth

Cruisers:
Blenheim (destroyer parent ship)
Dublin
Amethyst
Sapphire
Dartmouth

2nd Division:
Vengeance (flag)
Cornwallis

Triumph
Irresistible
Albion

3rd Division:
Bouvet
Charlemagne
Suffren
Gaulois
Massena

To come from home waters:
Swiftsure
Prince George
Canopus
Majestic
Lord Nelson and others

Hospital ships: *London, Canada*

Aeroplane ship: *Ark Royal*

15 British destroyers, four French destroyers, four submarines and four French submersibles; also, our Russian ally's contribution, the old cruiser *Askold*, known to the sailors as 'packet of Woodbines'. Our gunnery officer, somewhat cynically, used to say how pleased we all were if she hit the shore at all!

SUNDAY FEBRUARY 21ST. We had hoped to go into action and carry out our Order No. 1, but the wind was blowing gale force and the sea was rough, hence no day either for gunlaying or aeroplane ascent. We came to single anchor in the lee of Tenedos at 10 a.m.; it was blowing so hard one could not stand up on the fo'c'sle. We had divisions and church, in the battery, later.

During the forenoon hospital-ships *Canada* and *Soudan* came in as well as collier *Ingleside* and *Braemar Castle* with marines.

In the afternoon at 2 p.m. *Sapphire* came to anchorage towing submarine *B 11* (Lt Holbrook).

Since the end of 1914 our early B-class submarines had arrived at the Dardanelles. Their task was to penetrate the Narrows, enter the Sea of Marmara and there destroy Turkish shipping. Their difficulties were great; they were small ships and thus limited in their endurance for a protracted expedition away from base; also they had the hazardous voyage through the Narrows in overcoming the unpredictable swift-flowing currents and, lastly, negotiating their passage through the uncharted minefields. We all had the greatest admiration for these little ships and when Holbrook with B 11 sank the Turkish cruiser Messudieh and earned a V.C. we were thrilled.

In the spring of 1915 the three larger modern E-boats appeared and were able to have a far greater measure of success. They sank Turkish warships and supply ships; they blew up railways and showed themselves off Constantinople. Our interest in these submarines was immense. Their captains were our heroes: Nasmith with his First Lieutenant D'Oyly Hughes, Boyle, Stoker, Brodie and others were constantly in our minds and if they became overdue we prayed for their safety.

Their casualties were great. Of the twelve British and French submarines which entered or attempted to enter the Marmara, six were lost. Churchill writing in The World Crisis *describes their exploits as being 'The finest examples of submarine warfare of the whole World War'.*

We heard that German submarines had been preparing for the Mediterranean since the beginning of 1915, but very fortunately for us none had yet appeared at the Dardanelles.

At 5.20 p.m. we weighed and proceeded to sea, the 1st Division steering S38W, and turned 16 points at 1 a.m. When we had weighed, we could not turn up into the wind to get to our station although both engines were worked opposite ways, so in the end we had to turn stern to wind. (*Agamemnon* was a difficult ship to handle.)

MONDAY FEBRUARY 22ND. Owing to heavy sea running and wind, the whole Allied fleet came to anchor just off Tenedos village and harbour where there is a Turkish settlement, although the island itself is Grecian. There is a small breakwater outside the harbour and an old fort at the entrance; there were two British steam yachts in the harbour. On the land we could see many old windmills, ruins, etc. while the town lay in the gap.

There were many Greek sailing boats about, caiques I think they are called, and very pretty they look and can fairly nip along. At 10.15 a.m. collier *Remembrance* came alongside and we took in 845 tons; we finished at 4.15 p.m. after half an hour's interval for lunch — a hard day's work.

Queen Elizabeth left for Port Mudros (Lemnos) to get her turbines repaired by Malta dockyard men who have been sent out there, also to take in 1,800 tons of oil fuel. At 6 p.m. the whole Allied fleet weighed and proceeded to sea for the night. It still continued to blow hard from the south and set up a 'Channel sea' which made us batten down. During the day our minesweepers went in close to the forts and commenced sweeping operations; they also had a good look round and reported seeing many soldiers entrenched.

TUESDAY FEBRUARY 23RD. I kept the forenoon watch with Lt Hammet, who got into trouble with Fluter over a bad manoeuvre when we nearly rammed *Inflexible*.

At 10.15 a.m. the whole Allied fleet came to anchor in the lee of Tenedos (N. side), in the teeth of a gale force 7-8, and the devil of a short sea. *Queen Elizabeth* joined up before the squadron came to the anchorage.

After anchoring, all hands were employed working on the damaged main derrick, trying to unship it and replace it with the new one we took on board at Malta. It was a troublesome job as our boats had to be got out of the way first; it was not completed today, but it is hoped the job may be finished by tomorrow night.

At 6 p.m. the whole fleet weighed and proceeded to sea again; it has every appearance of being a dirty night, there being rain, lightning, thunder and wind of gale force. This is the fourth day that the gale has prevented us bombarding and so far there is no sign of the gale abating.

W/T signal from Admiral Malta: 'Learn from secret intelligence: *Goeben*'s repairs have been temporarily executed; she can now steam 17 knots.'

WEDNESDAY FEBRUARY 24TH. The 1st and 2nd Divisions steamed past Tenedos and came within 12,000 yds of the Entrance to the Dardanelles to have a look-round and see if the weather was clear enough; but, it being decided to the contrary, we all came to the anchorage under the lee of Tenedos at 11.20 a.m. The force of the wind has considerably decreased, the sea is not nearly so rough and it is a beautiful day. It seems a pity not to make use of it by bombarding the forts again, but the whole of Phase 1 (Reduction of Outer

Forts) must be carried out in one day and so the Admiral wants perfect weather to make sure of the job. Aeroplanes are to be used to ensure good spotting.

During the forenoon our cable-holder got jammed so we had to saw through our port anchor shackle; it was the only way to free it. During the afternoon the job of fitting the new derrick was completed, also the upper works of the ship were painted so as to give us a strange appearance.

At 3.30 p.m. *Dartmouth* came in flying the flag of Rear-Admiral Wemyss; she brought with her a small mail for us.

At 6 p.m. both our divisions weighed and proceeded to sea for the night; *Majestic* joined up at 6.50 p.m. It is a nice clear evening and there is every prospect of a good day's bombardment tomorrow.

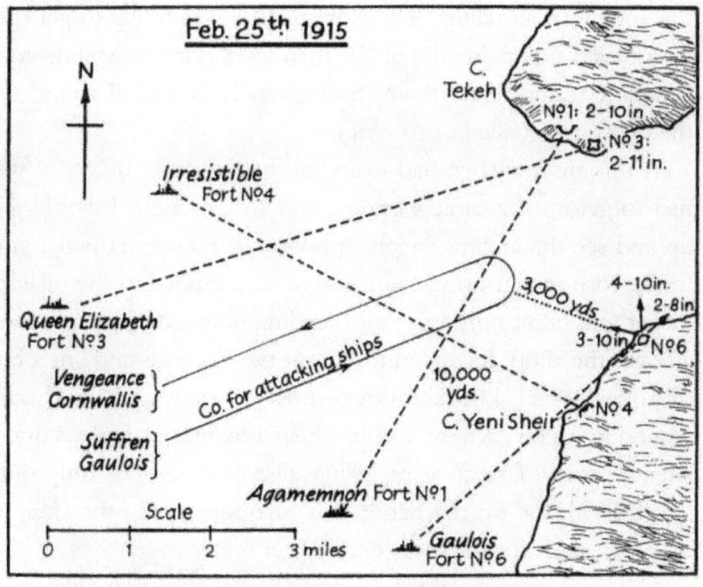

Bombardment of the Outer Forts

THURSDAY FEBRUARY 25TH. A beautiful day, very clear and an eventful day for me; one which I shall not forget.

We all steamed up to the coast in line ahead and there we each took up our appointed billets for the bombardment. *Agamemnon* came to single anchor at about 10 being 10,000 yds from No. 1 Fort and at 10.15 *Queen Elizabeth* opened fire on No. 3 Fort. *Gaulois* opened fire on No. 6 Fort and after half an hour I record that at 10.36 Fort fired 100 yds short. At 10.38 Fort fired and hit us amidships on main derrick-head, passing through the funnel and killed three men — Leading Seaman Small and Ordinary Seaman Mason and P.O. Worthington — and wounding very badly Yeoman Bishop, Gunner White, etc., nine altogether.

Meanwhile, as our after turret was not closed up (only the starb. 'nine-twos' being fired) I was strolling round recording the enemy shots falling. The Commander was trying to get the disengaged side painted, but the men were not very willing and I cannot really blame them. Seeing shells falling all round us the flagship signalled us to weigh.

At this moment we had everyone below deck; but now we had to get up the cable-workers, and so I thought I would go up and see the anchor weighed; however, no sooner had I got to the fore screen-door, than a large shell landed in the oilskin locker and burst right over me, sending lumps of iron splinters all over the shop. I saw red for about two seconds and got a bit of a blast which knocked down most of the men behind me, wounding many, whom I could hear groaning a few seconds later. Lumps of stuff were falling all round me but only one small bit hit me on the hand; only just penetrating the skin; it made me dash for the mess deck to get under cover.

While we were weighing, shots fell just over and then just short twice respectively, as we started going ahead and astern alternately with the engine. We were, however, hit five times during this evolution. Next hit was on S 2 turret on the side armour; this shell then went right through the upper deck, bursting in doing so and sending splinters everywhere around penetrating all our plating, light circuits, etc., but hitting no one, and it eventually landed in the marines' barracks. The third hit went through the foremost funnel and burst on the port foremost winch, smashing it to pieces and holing the flying deck. Fourth shot hit the topgallant mast 3 yds above the foretop, but only just scraped the outer wood off. Number 5 shot was an armour-piercing shell which holed the side on the aft deck in the ship's office, passed through two cabins, through main deck in the after hydraulic room causing a fire in a dangerous place, being between two magazines; however it was soon extinguished. Number 6 hit the 8-in. belt abreast of S 3 turret and failed to penetrate it.

At 10.45 we broke away and steamed out of range, but they still went on firing at us very close each time but never hitting again for we were soon beyond their range. We had been firing one gun per minute with our starboard battery.

At 11 a.m. the forts concentrated on French ship *Suffren*, shots falling all round her but only one actually hit her which knocked out and killed a turret's crew. Our shots were hitting earthworks, but their guns were still replying until one of our shots actually hit the gun and put it out of action although the gun still remained mounted. At 11.29 we again closed in to support *Gaulois*, firing one gun per minute and were now using 'lyddite' (high-explosive shell) at No. 1 Fort where one 24-cm (9.45-in.) gun is still replying. (Some of our 'lyddites' were bursting as soon as they were fired, but luckily they did not damage the gun at all.) At 11.50 the fort was firing hard at *Gaulois* while our shells were bursting all round their remaining gun and barracks in rear, range 8,000 yds. At 12.02 a good shot from *Queen Elizabeth* laid out their right gun, dismounting it altogether and then got another good shot and put the left-hand gun out of action, but we had already knocked out the crews previously.

At 12.25 we opened fire on No. 5 Fort, while *Gaulois* fired at No. 4 Fort which she soon hit. *Vengeance* and *Cornwallis* now proceeded to the entrance and did 'battle-practice run', firing at all forts from both sides at 3,000 yds and at noon *Queen Elizabeth* opened fire on No. 3 Fort. From now to 12.56 our starboard 'nine-twos' got in four good shots, *Cornwallis* and *Vengeance* firing vigorously on Forts 3 and 4.

I now got some lunch down in the gunroom and then came up and had a look at all our shell-holes, while the French ships began their battle-practice run and steamed in, like our two ships, and at 2.30 p.m. S 3 turret opened fire on No. 3 Fort again. Meanwhile *Charlemagne* and *Suffren* returned without receiving any reply to their fire. At 3.30 *Triumph* and *Albion* closed in and carried out their battle-practice run, firing directly at the guns of Forts 1 and 3. I saw *Triumph* knock one gun clear off its mounting in No. 1 Fort. About 4.12 single shots began to pitch all round *Gaulois*; these were eventually discovered to be from a howitzer firing behind the hill. The right gun at Fort 4 also opened fire on *Gaulois* to which she replied and we stood in to support her. We again went to Action Stations after half an hour's interval for tea and fired three rounds at the gun from close range and knocked it out of action, for I could see through my telescope that it was jammed and could not train. Finally we ceased fire at 5 p.m., having been in action six hours altogether and under direct fire for 20 minutes when shells were coming all round and hitting us. Had it not been for the fact that we first went ahead and then astern a few times before weighing the anchor we should have been hit more often.

It had been a fine sight to see *Q.E.*'s shells bursting at No. 6 Fort making tremendous smoke and scattering clouds of earth in all directions. Signal from Admiral to *Agamemnon*: 'Proceed in execution of previous orders.' We thereupon drew off and shaped a course for Tenedos coming to single anchor at 6.10 p.m. We then lowered our cutters and sent away seven seriously wounded men to hospital ship *Soudan*. The *Majestic*, which had been coaling all day, sent us a couple of mail bags.

At 6.20 p.m. *Queen Elizabeth* and *Inflexible* arrived and anchored, but the 2nd and 3rd Divisions, under Vice-Admiral de Robeck, carried on operations and entered the Dardanelles.

The effect of their shells that hit us was to make piercing holes rather than damage caused by burst, and hence they went through more plates by their momentum than they would have had they burst violently, although in the latter case they would have caused more havoc, wreckage and loss of life. We found there was no safe place under deck as their shells come down half vertically, owing to their high elevation and extreme range. Thus a well-pitched shell can easily penetrate into any magazine, as it has only two decks to go through and a 2-in. protected deck.

When Yeoman Bishop was hit by a large splinter from the first shell, he was reading a signal and continued to shout it out to the Captain when his leg had been almost shot off. At the same time another splinter went into the stomach of P.O. Worthington, wounding him very severely. When the stretcher party came up, Bishop refused to be touched before Worthington was taken down below. When he did get taken down below, he was most cheery all the time and even smoked a cigarette just after his leg had been amputated.

It is generally believed there were German gunners at No. 1 Fort, as they fired so well and stuck to their guns under heavy fire till their guns were knocked out by us.

The Turks fired altogether 56 shells at us of which seven were direct hits. We fired 123 rounds from 9.2-in. of which 12 were 'lyddite', remainder 'common', nearly all full-charge. Our casualties: three killed, nine seriously wounded.

The Admiral's signal indicates a demolition operation for tomorrow: '*Irresistible* and *Majestic* with mine-bumpers [we never knew what this meant] in place should be at the Entrance of Dardanelles at daylight and proceed inside and take up position one mile E.N.E. of Kum Kale, 1¾ miles east of Seddul Bahr to cover landing and take enemy in rear. Half the minesweepers are required and division of destroyers.'

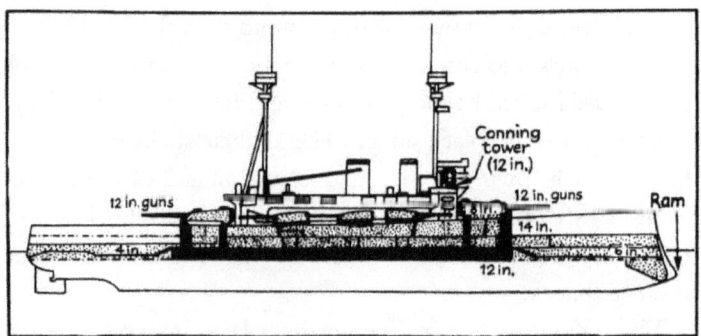

Agamemnon's armour protection ranged from 14-in. to 6-in. and made her a splendid floating fortress, but her turret roofing and protecting deck of only 2-in. plating made her vulnerable to plunging shellfire

FRIDAY, FEBRUARY 26TH. We remained at anchor off Tenedos all night and during the forenoon the hands were employed clearing up the wreckage and repairing damage and holes during yesterday's action. We had divisions and prayers.

During the latter I noticed what an impression yesterday's show had made on the men; for instead of the usual skylarking at prayers they all looked very solemn and quite melancholy, which I have never seen them look before.

Early in the morning the Union Castle liner, *Braemar Castle*, went in to land marines on the Seddul Bahr side. We also saw *Triumph* and *Vengeance* inside the Entrance with their minesweepers looking for mines. On the left side of the minaret a white flag was flying and we all came up and looked through our telescopes. *Dartmouth* was engaging a battery about 7,000 yds from us near a blockhouse on land; the battery replied but did not seem to hit her; there was also some bombarding by our ships inside the Entrance.

At 1.30 p.m. we weighed and proceeded to sea in order to bury our three dead; a very appropriate place — beautiful, clear, blue water. At 2.20 we started the burial service, the three bodies were borne on stretchers sewn up in their own hammocks and covered over with ensigns. They were committed to the deep in turn by sliding them down a gangplank into the sea whereupon they sank immediately. After this the rifle party under P.O. Warren fired three rounds after which there was the Last Post. On the whole it was very impressive even though it is war-time. One cannot realise disasters, or people getting killed, even though they aren't one's closest friends.

We then steamed back to the same anchorage south of Tenedos, and received the order to weigh again at 4.30 p.m. The 1st Division steamed in line ahead N.N.W. towards the south side of Imbros, north of Tenedos and at 6 p.m. *Lord Nelson* joined, taking station astern of us, now being no longer a flagship. We all came to anchor about 1½ miles from the shore off Imbros in 23 fathoms.

At 5.55 I saw two big magazine explosions in No. 3 Fort; the town we set ablaze last afternoon is still burning furiously and continued throughout last night.

Lord Nelson, just arrived on the station, brought us out a mail and I got two letters, one from home. Signal from *Lord Nelson* to us: 'Hurrah, hope you have left us a fort.' I think they will realise we have when they get to the Narrows.

During the forenoon today I had a look round the ship to see the damage done to us. Most shells went right through the thin ¼-in. plates without bursting or breaking up at all. The funnels had enormous great rents in them, also the flying deck. The only dangerous shell first came through the ship's side, through the two cabins, setting them ablaze and then it penetrated right through the 2-in. protected deck into the hydraulic-room; here, after smashing the engine, the shell buried itself in the mounting. Had the shell been 1 ft further outboard, it would have gone clean through the hydraulic-room deck into the 12-pdr magazine and then — probably the last of *Agamemnon*.

I was officially reported to the Admiralty as slightly wounded. I hope the parents will not get in a panic over it. *N.B.* At 8 p.m. a tremendous explosion took place at No. 6 Fort and I expect the Turks blew it up themselves.

SATURDAY FEBRUARY 27TH. We remained at anchor off Imbros all day. We had no divisions or physical drill and the hands had a 'make and mend' in the afternoon. It was pretty foggy most of the day and we could see nothing of any operations going on. At 2 p.m. *Vengeance* came to our anchorage from the Dardanelles. *Ocean* arrived off Tenedos.

SUNDAY FEBRUARY 28TH. It was again a wet and foggy

day, the wind blowing a gale of Force 8. On account of these conditions we spent another peaceful day at anchor off Imbros. During the forenoon we had divisions on the mess deck and a sit-down service afterwards, during which I slumbered. I went to lunch with Fluter for the first time, probably as it had come to his notice that I had been scratched by a splinter.

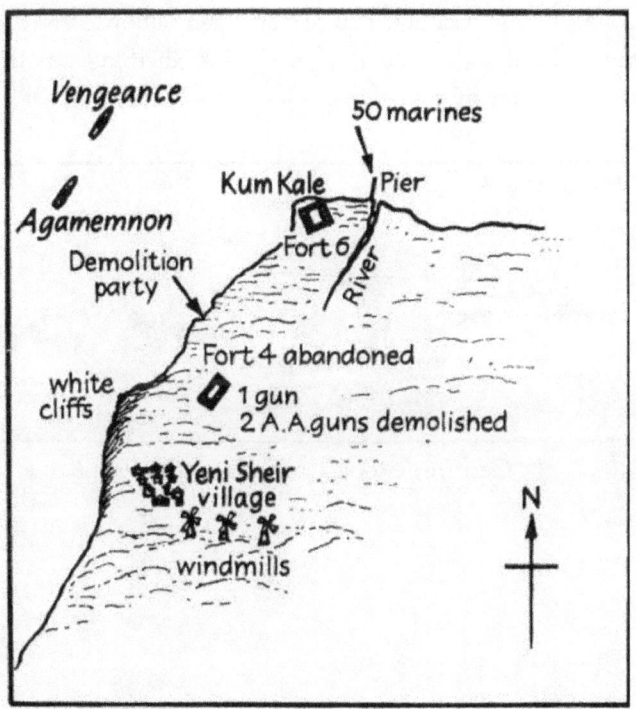

Demolition parties, Asiatic shore

During the afternoon the Admiral signalled: 'Learn through neutral agents at Sofia that 600 wounded Turks passed through Constantinople yesterday.' I expect a lot of these were townspeople wounded by our shells and fire, as the forts could hardly have sported 600 even if all were wounded. There must have been a good number killed while at their guns, which we have not heard of yet.

W/T signal from Admiral Malta stated: 'Four transports with 5,500 troops, 250 horses, field-kitchens and equipment will be arriving tomorrow or the next day. They carry one week's provisions with them for man and horse and a reserve of two months' supplies will be landed.'

Owing to the weather, marines and demolition party could not be landed today and I do not think anything was done today in the way of operations.

Lt Geoffrey Crookshank's sketch of Fort 6

THREE: LANDING OF DEMOLITION PARTIES

MONDAY MARCH 1ST. HMS *Swiftsure* came in and anchored off Imbros. Castle liner *Cawdor Castle*, with marines, also came to our anchorage. *Prince George* arrived at Tenedos and coaled all day.

At 5.15 p.m. we weighed and proceeded to Tenedos in order to take in coal tomorrow; we came to single anchor at 7 p.m. astern of *Prince George*.

I had to go away in the sea-boat to the collier and thence to the *Soudan* to see about our wounded. I saw all of them and they all seemed very cheery and much better, and were rather enjoying themselves there. I also had a yarn with other wounded people from the demolition parties of *Irresistible* and *Vengeance* and learnt that *Irresistible*'s torpedo lieut. fired the charge demolishing No. 1 Fort too soon, before they were all clear; thus many of them got wounded by flying bits of earth.

The *Vengeance* party which had been landed at Kum Kale had great difficulty on account of the Turkish snipers attacking them all the time. Germans were actually seen among the snipers; three of the party were injured and one was knocked *hors de combat* by a rifle bullet and fell down. The marine I was talking to went to his rescue, but too late, for a dirty Turk had knocked his head in with the butt end of a rifle, killing him.

Today *Albion* went 5 or 6 miles inside the Dardanelles and although she optimistically reported knocking out one fort, *Albion* was hit by howitzers (4-in.) and had four or five men wounded by splinters.

Our Admiral reported to Admiralty: '*Triumph, Ocean* and *Albion* in the Straits engaged Battery No. 8 and guns at White Cliffs. They were fired upon by five field guns and howitzers. In the evening seaplanes reported line of 17 mines across Straits on a line N.W. of Battery No. 8. Mines on the surface. Ships hit several times; casualties *Albion* one officer and four men wounded'.

TUESDAY MARCH 2ND. At 6 a.m. collier *Leamington* came alongside and we started to take in 630 tons, only using 1, 2 and 3 holds. 8 a.m. interval of ½ hr. for breakfast. We finished coaling at 12.10 p.m. and the collier shoved off but with 15 hands and six midshipmen in her; they could not get out of her owing to the heavy sea running and the increasing force of the wind made the hawsers and two wires carry away. Our coaling party were brought back the next day.

During the forenoon all the destroyers assembled near us for bread, as they have not had any for six days. Unfortunately we could not give them any and they looked just like a flight of hungry birds waiting for their daily ration. Fluter was senior officer and he made good use of his command by hoisting all sorts of objectionable signals to the other ships near us.

At 12.30 we weighed and proceeded round to the north side of the island, coming to single anchor between *Triumph* and *Majestic*; all the other ships had already left for the north side before us.

There was to have been a demolition party landed but owing to the swell, it could not be accomplished. The evening was very warm indeed, wind being light airs from the south. Operations inside the Dardanelles were continued as reported by signal to Admiralty: '*Canopus, Swiftsure, Cornwallis* entered Straits and engaged Fort 8, which now mounts seven guns.

Fort 8 opened heavy fire using 6-in. guns some of which fired 4,000 yds. Field batteries and howitzers also opened fire. Ships withdrew 5.30 p.m. after inflicting damage on Fort 8 which ceased fire at 4.50 p.m. All three ships were hit on several occasions, one man slightly wounded. Sweeping takes place tonight; seaplanes were unable to fly due to weather.'

We can see the Turkish searchlights from Tenedos quite plainly; they appear very bright.

WEDNESDAY MARCH 3RD. Admiralty has announced that our ships have entered the Dardanelles and are now 8 miles up. In my opinion this is rather exaggerated as only destroyers have been that far.

Suddenly, between 7 and 8 a.m. the wind shifted right round to the N.E. making it bitterly cold — worse than in England. At 9.30 a.m. it was blowing so hard that all the 1st Division weighed and proceeded to the south side of Imbros which is just as mountainous as its north side, the mountain peaks being snow-clad. There is very deep water here right close in and we must have been ¾ mile from land. The two transports came with us, also *Amethyst* and a destroyer. In the afternoon I had to go away exercising boat's crew in sailing, etc. During the Dog Watches we had a splendid game of deck hockey; it was a glorious sunset and the wind has again abated and shifted round to the east and it is now quite warm.

Weather too bad to begin operations until 2 p.m. when firing on Fort 8 and concealed guns was resumed by *Irresistible*, *Albion*, *Prince George* and *Triumph*. Concealed guns appeared to be less aggressive and ships are dealing with them with more certainty. Progress is being made though weather disorganised operations. Seaplanes flying in the afternoon made useful reconnoitring, locating permanent batteries and encampments.

Reported that parties from *Irresistible*, who were surveying camber at Seddul Bahr, found and destroyed a battery of six modern field-guns which were under arches of the old fort. At 9.30 p.m. signal to *Agamemnon*: 'You will be required to cover landing force at Kum Kale tomorrow. Provide two cutters which will be towed by *Irresistible*'s picket-boat. Prepare to weigh 5.30 a.m.'

THURSDAY MARCH 4TH. A beautiful day, no wind and a cloudless sky. We weighed at 7.30 a.m. and proceeded in company with *Lord Nelson*, also four 'Beagle'-class destroyers containing 250 men (about) and two Castle liners following. *Inflexible* also followed a long way astern.

At about 9.30 *Lord Nelson* suddenly opened fire on a red object in the water, looking like a mine; we accordingly opened fire with our 12-pdrs as well and altered course so as to hit it. We had everyone under cover so that the mine should not injure anyone if it burst and then blazed away with 20 rounds of 'practice' and at last hit it, but to everyone's surprise it sank peacefully. Signal from *Agamemnon* to Admiral: 'Have sunk mine.' Reply: 'Hope you have not sunk *Irresistible*'s mark-buoy.' Everyone except the Captain was amused!

At 9.50 a.m. we were inside the Entrance and conformed to instructions received previously for landing demolition parties.

'Off Kum Kale: Boats to muster astern of *Irresistible* by 9 a.m. Each ship to provide one steamboat, one pinnace and two cutters or pinnace and three cutters. Three destroyers to form a screen to north. One destroyer to attend W/T office. *Lord Nelson* and Ark *Royal*, minesweepers to remain outside Entrance as required.'

On the Gallipoli side were: *Ocean*, off No. 3 Fort, in charge, with boats mustered astern, *Majestic* off Morto Bay, *Lord Nelson* off Cape Helles.

We immediately lowered both cutters which were manned with marines, extra provisions, etc. They went to the destroyers, already full of troops and were towed in by *Irresistible*'s picket-boat. Meanwhile, *Agamemnon* and all other ships had started firing at the villages on both shores — Kum Kale and Seddul Bahr — so as to clear the place of snipers as much as possible.

As soon as our cutters had reached the shore they had a fierce musketry fire opened on them by snipers concealed in the ruins; they also fired on our boats with their Nordenfeldt guns. Luckily no one was hit before landing, but as soon as they mustered on top of the pier they had to lie flat; some of them were wounded and they had to make dashes to get clear of the pier and behind cover. We were watching all this through our glasses and could see our poor devils getting a rotten time from these snipers who could not be seen. Our marines were trying to support the *Lord Nelson*'s demolition party to demolish Fort No. 4 as there is still one big gun mounted there which is jammed on one bearing. We continued firing our 12-pdrs at Yeni Sheir village and at the cemetery, where there were Turks concealed with their guns. *Irresistible* and *Cornwallis*, firing on Kum Kale village, unluckily landed one shell on their demolition party.

At Seddul Bahr, *Ocean* opened fire to disperse the Turks, who were well entrenched and offered strong opposition to our men. At 10.20 we fired at the beach near cemetery and at 10.50, joined by *Inflexible*, *Agamemnon* opened fire on a gun to the right of Yeni Sheir village. We saw a seaplane go up from *Ark Royal* and when over Aren Kioi they fired shrapnel at her which we could see by the little clouds of smoke. Meanwhile another aeroplane ascended. 11.20 we made good use of our 12-pdrs on the left of Yeni Sheir village as there were a lot of Turks in the houses apparently spotting; also spotting from windmills and the church, so we fired at all these places in turn and knocked down a few jolly fine houses, cottages, etc. [*The diary now records further bombarding of the targets on the Asian shore especially near Yeni Sheir village where the enemy was concealed and continually molesting the work of our demolition parties whose task could not be completed until late afternoon. The diary then continues:*]

At 3.30 heard firing on ridge to left of windmills, which was our soldiers engaging enemy troops entrenched behind wire entanglements which we could see. Soldiers and demolition party were now retreating along the beach taking cover where possible, and I could see many of them fall and then try and raise themselves and move on, being helped by others. Thus they went on in small groups retiring along the beach having to lie flat and then run hard and then duck again. I could see the bullets splashing in the water by the shore.

At 4.30 we ceased firing, but five destroyers and *Amethyst* carried on shelling windmills and houses, and at 4.45 we opened fire on the same objects. At 4.47 P 2 opened fire on same howitzer as before and on more houses and buildings and kept a heavy fire on the top of cliff so as to enable our men to retreat unmolested as much as possible. We watched them through the telescope the whole time retiring along the beach.

Signal from R.A.: 'Intend sending in boats to rescue wounded officers and men at the base of Fort 4. Shall carry on operations after dark.' At 6 p.m. enemy gun fired three shots ahead of us apparently at transport which eventually cleared out of their range; they did not fire any more although they had our range. We carried on firing our 12 pdrs at the cliff after dark till 7 p.m. and were then ordered to cease firing and wait for our boats to return. Meanwhile, our wounded were being brought back from the pier at Kum Kale all the afternoon; they got a hot reception there too.

Our soldiers had had to leave their Maxims on the pier so volunteers had to rescue them. All our 2nd cutter crew volunteered, but only Leading Seaman Squires of the 1st cutter; the crew had to be completed by *Nelson*'s. They went in and rescued the guns without being hurt although they were under heavy fire at the time. Some of them landed and had a whack with wounded soldiers' rifles. The destroyers eventually got up a volunteer crew to man a couple of whalers which went in aided by searchlights and rescued wounded from the beach.

It was a very unsuccessful day; only four Nordenfeldts destroyed and it cost the lives of 19 men, 23 wounded and three missing of the soldiers alone, not including the casualties of *Nelson*'s demolition party. At 8 p.m. cutters returned and were hoisted aboard much to the satisfaction of the crews.

Altogether we fired 700 rounds of 12-pdrs and 18 of 9.2-in. (12 'common' and six 'lyddite'); some 'tracers' were fired by mistake!

Agamemnon and *Inflexible* proceeded to sea for the night. Army transports arrived Port Mudros: *Nizam*, *Suffolk*, *Heverna*, *Iowa* and *Magda*.

FRIDAY MARCH 5TH. At 9 a.m. we were off Imbros anchorage and were ordered to watch Nos. 1 and 4 Forts at the Entrance. Arriving there at 10.30 we prepared for immediate action. *Irresistible*, *Cornwallis* and *Albion* went inside, the latter ship spotting for *Queen Elizabeth*, which was firing at the Narrows' forts from over the peninsula by Yeni Tekir.

According to the spotting corrections, *Q.E.*'s firing was very good and should have destroyed a good bit of the forts on the left side of the Narrows.

We expected that we should land men in our cutters again like yesterday, but as we had received no further orders, Willis and I asked the Commander to tell Fluter we wanted to go, as other 'snotties' had gone in *their* cutters from other ships yesterday. Nothing happened at all during the forenoon, but during the afternoon batteries started firing at *Cornwallis* and at 2 p.m. *Cornwallis* opened fire to the right of barracks behind Kum Kale. At 2.30 p.m. many shells splashed all round *Irresistible* probably from Fort No. 7 which we could not see; these were big stuff by the splashes. At 3.15 p.m. we opened fire on battery behind Kum Kale firing five rounds which silenced their guns.

We left the battery firing at some of the French sweepers which had to draw off, and we then proceeded to Tenedos and anchored on the north side.

All day I had had my glass trained on the beach, but failed to discover any sign of the Turks; I could see only some of our demolition party's 16¼-lb tins (explosive charges) lying on the beach near the cemetery.

Signal from *Soudan* stated that boy Mocket has died of his wounds; he was only fifteen a day before he got wounded and he seemed so cheery when I saw him in bed on board the hospital ship *Soudan* a few days ago.

Triumph and *Swiftsure* left with six minesweepers for operations at Smyrna.

It would seem that up to this stage of the campaign there could have been reason for optimism. We had destroyed the outer defences and landed demolition parties at little cost in ships and men. Now we were starting on

Phase Two of the plan: sweeping the minefields and reducing the defences up to the Narrows.

SATURDAY MARCH 6TH. Weighed at 6 a.m. and proceeded straight to Gaba Tepe to support *Queen Elizabeth* which was to fire over the Peninsula at the forts at the Narrows. Yesterday when she was firing they brought up field guns and howitzers and hit her several times mostly with 12-pdrs.

Being only 300 yds from shore I expected to be fired on any moment, and at 11 a.m. all of a sudden a shot pitched 50 yds short of us and immediately all the guns' crews made a bolt for their turrets or under armour; I must confess I did the same. A few of our 9.2-in. shells, fired at a house and some trees, cleared out some Turks who were spotting for their howitzers or batteries. After two more shots landing close astern we fell out from Action Stations for dinner, and afterwards when we were peacefully lying about on the quarterdeck two more big shells suddenly pitched astern — where they came from none could tell, but a ship could be seen steaming up and down the Dardanelles above the Narrows, and it could have been her firing at us.

Once more we went to Action Stations and fired 9.2-in. guns at pretty well nothing, and then packed up at 3.15 leaving *Queen Elizabeth* with shots all round her. She had to weigh anchor and shift berth, having fired only eight rounds of her 15-in., besides a fair amount of 6-in. at concealed batteries, which our aeroplanes, owing to engine trouble, could not locate.

On the way back to Tenedos at 4 p.m. we sighted what I thought were *Tiger* and *Indomitable* but they turned out to *be dummies*. When I first saw '*Tiger*' she resembled the proper ship exactly except for having too much freeboard. This was the only way one could distinguish their disguise in the distance.

They kept a long way from every ship and also from the land. We had no idea they were coming out here and do not yet know the reason. We learnt later that the former ship was apparently the old *Prinzessin Cecilie* (Norddeutsche Lloyd) captured as a prize.

These dummy warships, described in a subsequent signal as 'special service ships Nos. 11 and 14', were merchant ships cleverly disguised by the Belfast shipyards to deceive the enemy into reporting them as British battle-cruisers. Later, we learnt that the intention was to delude the Germans into thinking we were depleting the Grand Fleet in order to provide more warships to back up the Dardanelles expedition, or possibly to discourage Germany's battle-cruiser Goeben *from making a sortie from Constantinople.*

One of these ships was later sunk by a U-boat whose captain must have been astonished to see the surviving crew clinging to the floating wooden turrets, when the ship sank beneath the waves. But one vessel, Orion, *survived to be sunk by us later to form a much-needed shelter at our advance base, Kephalo, on the island of Imbros.*

We came to anchor north of Tenedos at 5.30 p.m. and I was sent away in the 2nd cutter to *Inflexible* and *Q.E.* for letters and spuds.

FOUR: PRELIMINARY BOMBARDMENT OF NARROWS' FORTS

SUNDAY MARCH 7TH. Being the sabbath we were hoping to have a peaceful day at last, but at 11 a.m. we were informed it was not to be so. We had the usual Sunday divisions and then church on the quarterdeck. Meanwhile, Fluter was ordered to the flagship to get Orders, which he explained when he returned on board, having stopped the parson in the middle of a miserable sermon. He said that *Agamemnon* and *Lord Nelson* were to go right inside to bombard the Chanak forts at the Narrows during this afternoon. This was a bit more than we had bargained for and we expected to get a very thin time as the Chanak forts are by far the most powerful we have yet to encounter.

At 11.10 a.m. we weighed and proceeded in company with *Lord Nelson* towards the Straits. We cleared for Immediate Action and then had an early lunch. We went to General Quarters at 12.15 p.m., not feeling altogether comfortable. We met the four French ships which were to support us by firing at Nos. 7 and 8 Forts and field guns and howitzers.

We opened fire with our fore turret at 12.35, being 15,000 yds from No. 13 Fort. The Turks then opened fire on us and soon picked up the range, shots falling all around us. Number 13 had two 11-in. guns, four 9.5-in. and a couple of mortars, which were extremely difficult to hit. Number 19 Fort, which *Lord Nelson* was firing at, was a large target on the right bank and had two 14-in. and seven 9.2-in. guns. It started firing at us as well as at *Lord Nelson*; then some stray howitzers at 7 and 8 Forts started firing at us. At 12.44 the first shell hit us forward starb. side in net-shelf thence passing through the deck and after making a big hole passed into E.R.A.'s mess but no further; it was probably a 9.2-in. or perhaps smaller. At 2.45 another shell hit us port side opposite fore turret. It made a big hole in the side and smashed up the seamen's Heads, the splash of it drenching everyone in the conning tower. There were enormous splashes all round us as high as the foretop, nearly, and it was only by good manoeuvring of the ship and keeping up 14 knots and zigzagging that we avoided being hit more often; Fort 13 often got 'straddles', *Lord Nelson* getting a very thin time with huge splashes all round her; she was very lucky not being hit yet. We steamed round in a triangle all the time firing salvos with the whole broadside, full charge at all guns; it was really fine to feel the ship tremble. At 1.10 the forts were firing salvos; we can feel the old *Nellie* firing close to us and the French ships fairly plonking away with their 5.5 guns for all they were worth. Number 19 started firing salvos and straddling *Nellie* at 1.25. We closed in to 11,000 yds and gave No. 13 the whole broadside; we would then open to 13,000 yds and fire one turret at a time. At 1.26 we were hit aft on the quarterdeck port side probably by a big howitzer or a long-range 12-in. or 9.2-in. which burst on striking the upper deck, wrecking the wardroom, and then the gunroom, wrecking a lot of that too, including the gramophone. The hole in the upper deck was a yard square. Other shots hit our armour belt, but they made no impression and only bounced off into the ditch again; we could feel a dull thud as they hit us. 2.05. Salvo from Chanak forts very close to *Lord Nelson*, and hit her at 2.27 on the flying deck, splinters going into conning tower, wounding captain, commander and chief quartermaster, all slightly. At 2.14 left gun of No. 13 Fort was put out of action and fired no more; also No. 19 Fort which ceased firing.

By 2.30 only small shells occasionally fired at us now but no more hit us. At 2.50 French ships firing at Aren Kioi village. Two guns now appear to be out of action in Fort 13 and nothing more replying to us.

At 3.09 p.m. ceased firing and proceeded with *Lord Nelson* out of Dardanelles at slow speed. Howitzers' shots still falling near French ships but they were not hit, though very close at the time. As soon as it was safe we 'fell out' and there was, as usual, a general scramble to pick up the bits of shell which were very small this time as they all burst properly.

At 4.20 p.m. we arrived at Tenedos and anchored on north side. *Lord Nelson* is leaking badly and some bunkers are reported to be flooded. During the day we had fired 145 9.2-in. full charge and 80 12-in. full charge. No casualties at all for us today, and though it was impossible to estimate how much they fired it must have been a good lot more than 100 shots. We were not sorry when it was over for we had extraordinary good luck not being seriously hit; while their shooting was very good. Splinters today were very bad, for they used quite a different type of shell from those fired by the Outer Forts.

After dinner we had a great scrap with the wardroom, who started pouring water through the holes in the deck on top of us, and so we retaliated with water-pistols.

MONDAY MARCH 8TH. At Tenedos. At 8.15 a.m. collier *Tabarka* came alongside and we started taking in 500 tons, finished by 11.30. She had double derricks and double winches for each hold and I worked the fore winch most of the time. Afternoon spent washing down. Early, *Lord Nelson* sailed for Port Mudros, probably so that the repair-ships can get to work on her.

Reported that one of our aeroplanes fell into the sea from a height of 2,000 ft, but luckily only the machine got absolutely smashed; the pilot and observer got cut about and badly shaken, having to be taken to the *Soudan*. Another machine sank alongside *Ark Royal*, as the floats leaked after being hit by rifle-fire from Kum Kale. Another seaplane reported sunk at Malta, so now they have only two good machines left out of the original five.

TUESDAY MARCH 9TH. At Tenedos. Nothing much happened all day; after divisions we hoisted out the galley for the Captain's benefit. In the Dog Watches we had an excellent game of deck-hockey for a couple of hours.

WEDNESDAY MARCH 10TH. My Middle Watch on decoding duty. Signal from Admiral to Admiralty: 'Mobile guns on the Asiatic shore can be silenced only by guns mounted on Gallipoli, and meanwhile attack on Narrows was at a standstill. Their searchlights could not be put out by destroyers.'

Later, we learnt of a signal from Admiralty, presumably initiated by Churchill: '— greater risks to justify loss of ships and men if success cannot be achieved without; — to overwhelm forts at Narrows at decisive range by greatest number of guns.'

These signals seemed as though the Admiral was not optimistic about making quick progress, while Admiralty in London was urging him to press on. They brought home to some of us that all was not well!

During the forenoon *Inflexible* and *Queen Elizabeth* sailed for Port Mudros, followed later by *Agamemnon* arriving at 6.30 p.m.

Meanwhile, the wind and sea got up from the S.W., preventing some Greek trading boats alongside us from getting back to their coast at Tenedos. When told to shove off from us, they protested, saying that they would drift down to Turkey and get their heads cut off.

Our mails — 19 bags — were sent over by Lord Nelson *on arrival. It was important for the morale of our expeditionary force to have a quick mail service from England. Mail was soon organised to come out overland to reach Taranto in about four days and here it was transferred to the fast P & O 'Express steamer'* Isonzo *(built in 1898 for the Overland Route to India — a ten-day service — when she operated on split-second timing between Brindisi and Alexandria).*

These days, conveying our Dardanelles mail to Malta in 24 hours, Isonzo *would then transfer it to one of the Khedeval mail-steamers, which, steaming at 17 knots, reached Mudros 2½ days later. These mailboats, being so fast, were seldom escorted, but they had some near-misses from enemy torpedoes.*

Allowing for occasional repairs, these ships were able to maintain a mail service from England in about 8-10 days.

THURSDAY MARCH 11TH. We embarked 21 rounds of T.N.T. 9.2-in. shell, said to be very violent.

A signal from the Admiral asking for volunteers among commissioned, subordinate and warrant officers to take on minesweeping in the Dardanelles when called upon to do so. Most of us put in our names. It is believed to be for the purpose of stiffening morale of the trawler crews.

FRIDAY MARCH 12TH. At 7 a.m. the Cunarder *Franconia* and *Royal George* arrived, the former with General Paris, and the naval brigade in both ships.

A 'sweeping trawler' anchored 50 yds off *Agamemnon* to enable our carpenters to repair the hole made by a 6-in. shell during the last night's sweeping. Her skipper told us they were constantly under fire and sweeping was not successful. Another trawler, when hauling in her sweep, exploded four mines she had gathered; the trawler sank, but the crew were saved. He added that these mines were not as violent as North Sea mines, for they only shoot up a column of water about 30 ft, but make no flame.

A lazy day for us ashore playing football.

SATURDAY MARCH 13TH. My morning watch, and so cold that I shivered. *Alnwick Castle* came in at 9 a.m. and *Somali* earlier, with airship on board; both have large pontoons for landing purposes.

During the afternoon we landed a recreation party and another one at 4 p.m.; unfortunately, I was unable to land having to keep an afternoon watch.

FIVE: MINESWEEPING — OUR INADEQUATE EQUIPMENT

As regards the obstructing mines in the Dardanelles Admiralty had informed us of 10 lines stretching across the Straits between a position about 8 miles inside the Entrance and the Narrows. It was known that some lines were laid at the end of the last year and believed that many more had been laid early this year.

To sweep the minefields the fleet had at first been provided with, I think, eight North Sea trawlers, capable of an effective sweeping speed against the Dardanelles current of up to 3 knots over the land. As the Admiral stressed on more than one occasion, this was quite inadequate, and our lack of suitable minesweepers was soon holding up operations.

SATURDAY MARCH 13TH. Signal received stating trawlers with volunteer crews had been sweeping up the Straits; this described how the Turks let the trawlers get well up the Straits and then switched on one searchlight only for a short time, firing all the while, and thus preventing our destroyer from getting a chance to hit the searchlight. Tonight, the cruiser *Amethyst*, while supporting minesweepers near the Narrows, was hit by two shells bursting in the stokers' bathroom starb. side forward, immediately killing 22 men and wounding severely 28 others, all sleeping in the flat.

Minesweeping continued against ever-increasing opposition from the enemy. The Turks, now supported by their German allies, not only increased their firepower and searchlights but apparently used them with greater efficiency. With a battleship or cruiser in support our trawlers were nevertheless opposed by such terrific gunfire that, certainly on one occasion, they had to slip their sweeps and return from the Straits. Destroyer Scorpion, *commanded by Lt-Comdr. Cunningham (later Admiral Lord Cunningham) was frequently in support of the trawlers; he describes in* A Sailor's Odyssey *how the trawlers steamed up to Kephez Point then got out their sweeps and swept downstream with the current. They got a tremendous battering, and though the support ships blazed away at the searchlights they were difficult to knock out.*

Having barely made progress with minesweeping, the attack on the Narrows was at a standstill. At the Admiralty Churchill records in World Crisis *that the First Sea Lord informed him, 'The more I consider the Dardanelles the less I like it. No matter what happens it is impossible to send out anything more — not even a dinghy — and why a hostile submarine has not appeared is a wonder.' This we learnt later.*

SUNDAY MARCH 14TH. A beautiful day. Sunday divisions; then stokers mustered by 'Open List', followed by church on the quarterdeck.

Our ships have been bombarding Bulair, on the isthmus at the head of the Gulf of Xeros, a garrisoned town with fort and earthworks, mostly a survival from Crimea days. It seems possible that our troops may be landed here.

At present there are always two of our battleships inside the entrance of the Dardanelles keeping an eye on the forts and batteries.

At 2.45 p.m. weighed and proceeded in company with *Lord Nelson* arriving north Tenedos at 6.15 p.m., *Queen Elizabeth* arrived an hour later having again had engine trouble. On the way we passed close to the two 'dummy ships' and we could plainly make out their old liner hulls and patchwork.

MONDAY MARCH 15TH. W/T signal stating bad boiler explosion in *Dartmouth*, totally wrecking a boiler room, four killed, seven wounded (all of whom died later). She came and anchored astern of us at 11 a.m.

W/T signal informing Admiralty that our present minesweepers can only make 1-2 knots against the strong current — hence are an easy target. Six fast sweepers should be coming out from England, also six French; *Inflexible* is bringing out sweeping gear for the 'River'-class destroyers. Sweeping is holding back the whole operation.

Signal stating *Agamemnon* to provide one picket-boat armed with rifles, ammunition and grapnel for sweeping mines located in Kephez Bay. We (i.e. the seven of us) cut for the bloke who was to go, and of course Willis got it. We then had to provide one Lieutenant or midshipman for volunteer sweeper, and Mr Crookshank and Pearson won the toss; I again had no luck.

Signal from Admiralty stating that Turkey had said she would not necessarily respect British, French or Russian hospital ships. (Probably because we frequently change their function before the Turkish government can be notified.) Also, they named two of their ships which are no longer hospital ships.

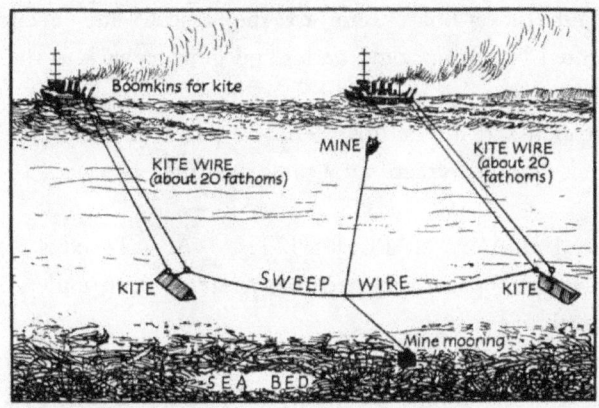

Minesweeping 'Beagle'-class destroyers

TUESDAY MARCH 16TH. At 4 a.m. Willis and Mr Holmes returned safely from the night's minesweeping in the picket boat having been 'creeping' up at Kephez Pt. and were under fire a good bit with powerful searchlights on them for much of the time; Nordenfeldts were continually firing on them. 6.30 a.m. Pearson and Mr Crookshank returned from their sweeping having been at it all night. They were 'flagship' and so led the line, but four of the sweepers deserted or got lost on the way in; they were not much under fire although searchlights played on them all the time; the 'flagship' rammed a destroyer on the way back.

At 8 a.m. collier *King John* came alongside and we began taking in 420 tons, which was accomplished after many mishaps: firstly the heel of No. 3 derrick carried away, another winch broke down, end of cylinder of No. 2 blew out, etc.; it took 3½ hours to get it all in.

At 4.15 p.m. *Triumph* and *Swiftsure* arrived. I took Mr Crookshank and Pearson to *Q.E.* for sweeping again tonight. At 6 p.m. a seaplane was taxying along the water when a float broke and so she heeled right over to 90° and started sinking, but our picket-boat went to the rescue and eventually prevented her from going under and got her back to the *Ark Royal* when she was hoisted in.

Garrioch and Mr Pettman left at 7 p.m. for the picket-boat which is going to 'creep' for a cable near the Narrows.

WEDNESDAY MARCH 17TH. At Tenedos. Our minesweeping party returned safely having been under heavy fire much of the night.

Vice-Admiral Carden has gone on the sick-list, probably owing to worry and he was taken to Malta in the *Minerva* which left during the forenoon. Vice-Admiral de Robeck hoisted his flag in the *Queen Elizabeth* at noon. (He is subsequently referred to as the Admiral.)

At 7 a.m. *Inflexible* came in bringing with her sweeping gear for destroyers intended for 'River'-class, but it was the more powerful 'Beagle'-class which actually swept mines); she was 1,150 tons of coal short and started taking it in immediately. In the afternoon I had to take away the cutter with boys and we sailed round the squadron.

My First Dog, during which *Dartmouth* and *Phaeton* (light cruisers) came in at 4 p.m., the latter with General Sir Ian Hamilton and his staff from France; later she sailed for Port Mudros.

Hamilton could hardly have realised that he had arrived on the eve of the Navy's final attack on the Narrows.

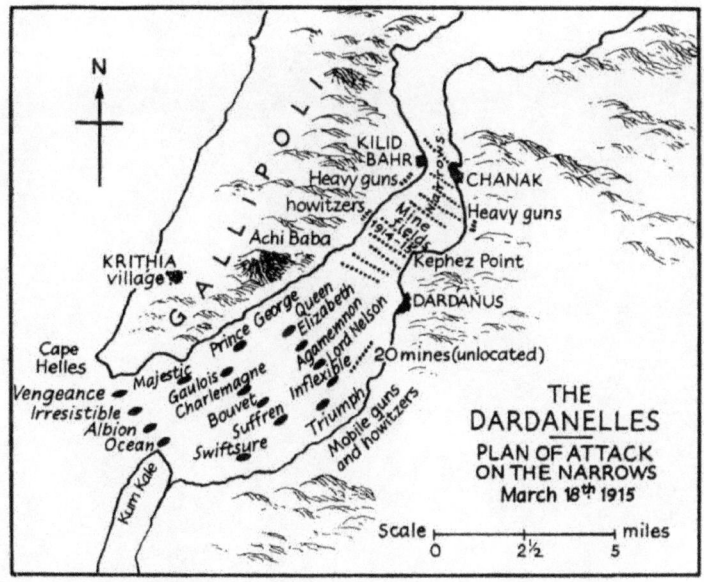

Plan of attack on the Narrows, March 18th 1915

At 5.15 p.m. we sent away picket-boat towing all boats except 1st cutter (i.e. launch, pinnace, 2nd cutter, galley and gig). The object of hoisting out all boats is to avoid their being smashed in tomorrow's bombardment, carrying out Phases 3 and 4, when the whole squadron is to attack the Narrows. The great concerted attack at last. All unnecessary gear is to be got rid of now.

The picket-boat then left as 'flagship' for the night's minesweeping operations with our crew, but not with our officers; the Commander would not let any of us go although approached twice on the matter. Our picket-boat is only to act as pilot for the rest of the flotilla.

SIX: FLEET'S FINAL ATTACK ON THE NARROWS

THURSDAY MARCH 18TH. A day to be remembered with regret by the Allied squadron out here and by the Navy in general. At 8.30 a.m. 1st Division *Prince George* and *Triumph* weighed and proceeded to the Entrance of the Dardanelles for the proposed reduction of the Narrows' forts.

The scheme for this reduction was roughly this: *Inflexible*, *Lord Nelson*, *Agamemnon* and Queen *Elizabeth* were to attack respectively Forts Nos. 19, 20, 13 and 17 at 14,000 yds and when they showed signs of sufficiently relaxing their fire we were to close in to 8,000 yds while the French ships were to close in to 3,000 and destroy remaining guns by direct fire. Meanwhile minesweepers were to clear a passage 9,000 yds wide in Sari Sigler Bay to enable ships to fire from there at the remaining forts at the Narrows.

At 10.30, proceeding into Straits, *Agamemnon* taking the honourable position in the line, preceded by three destroyers. At 11 a.m. howitzer battery on Asiatic side opened fire on the destroyers and on us as well.

The following was our Admiralty intelligence on the strength of the enemy defences:

Fort 13: 4 9.4-in., 2 11-in.

Fort 17: 4 6-in., 2 8.5-in., 11 9.8-in., 2 11-in.

Fort 19: 7 9.4-in., 2 14-in.

Fort 20: 6 6-in., 7 9-in., 2 11-in., 2 14-in.

At 11.12 the Narrows was in sight and at 11.36 the *Queen Elizabeth* opened fire on No. 19 Fort. We opened fire on No. 13 with fore turret, range 14,000 yds. Two minutes later *Lord*

Nelson and *Inflexible* opened fire on the Narrows with the fore turrets, all four of us being bows up stream and stationary with regard to the land. The big forts were not replying, but concealed batteries at Kephez Pt. and all over the place were firing; for we could detect them. At 11.44 shots began falling between us and *Queen Elizabeth* and then all round us from howitzer batteries. We saw *Queen Elizabeth* hit abreast of B-turret and a big explosion near No. 13 Fort with large volumes of black and yellow smoke. A minute later a salvo fell all round *Lord Nelson* and then shots falling very near us, some close alongside, making the ship vibrate by water hammering. At 12.17 saw *Inflexible* hit on fore bridge and *Lord Nelson* getting a warm time. At 12.22 salvos of three or four shots 50 yds off our port beam continue to fall now all round us, probably from 8-in. howitzers which we could not locate; they burst on striking the water very close, making the ship shake like blazes. I thought the after turret was going by the board for it lifted clean off its seating and shook everyone inside. More shots hit us; shell burst just outside our turret; saw all the flash inside and much noise; it must have been a high-explosive shell. At 1.06, shot hit the conning-tower, others close, but we now cleared out of range and as shots fell astern of us they started to practise on *Lord Nelson*.

Meanwhile, the French battle-squadron, which had steamed close towards the Narrows, was withdrawing at about 2 p.m. when *Bouvet* suddenly heeled over and quickly started to sink; she disappeared by the stern in about 1½-2 minutes. When she apparently hit the bottom, she remained stationary for a few seconds and then she disappeared altogether. *Gaulois* and *Suffren* then came over at full speed to pick up survivors, also destroyers and some picket-boats; they only picked up about 64, of which our boat got four. *Bouvet* had evidently had a shot in her magazine. *Gaulois* then appeared to have struck a mine; she soon cleared out and later ran herself aground on Rabbit Island in a sinking condition.

At 2.15 our 2nd Division ships *Vengeance*, *Albion*, *Ocean* and *Irresistible* now closed in to about 10,000 yds, the big forts firing at them; No. 19 Fort firing three or four big guns, No. 13 firing two guns. At 2.30 shots fell between us and *Queen Elizabeth*, who was hit twice; we were replying all the time with our 9.2-in. guns singly. At 3.05 explosion again seen in No. 13 Fort. At 3.30 big shots from Fort 19 were straddling *Irresistible* and soon after, 2nd Division was ordered to extend their distance from enemy.

Minesweepers were now being fired at by shrapnel during their minesweeping and half an hour later *Lord Nelson* reported mine to starb., and all picket-boats engaged it.

At 4.10 *Inflexible* struck a mine in forward torpedo flat, drowning 41 men; before this she had a fire on her bridge and foretop, killing several men and their gunnery lieutenant. At the beginning of the action she had lost her picket-boat after the crew had already abandoned her.

At 4.15 *Irresistible* could now be seen to be hit by many shells and listed over to starboard. We kept firing one gun at a time slowly at Fort 13 aided by *Queen Elizabeth*, but the fort still fired two guns, and *Irresistible* continued to be under fire and seemed to be down by the stern. Destroyers now closed in to her and took off all except a volunteer crew of about 20 (mostly officers) in order to get a hawser ready for taking her in tow. I watched all the proceedings through my glass and could see shells landing on their quarterdeck causing some casualties, also killing the boat lowerers so that the cutter's after-fall parted throwing them in the sea; shells pitching among the rescuers, but all destroyers and picket-boat stuck to their job well under the heavy fire. At 5 p.m. *Ocean* was ordered to take *Irresistible* in tow.

A picket-boat now passed and shouted to Mr Gardner and myself who had our heads out of the turret hatch: 'Mine right ahead of you.' We passed the news through to the conning-tower and we went 'full astern'. (Everyone in the turret treated it as quite a joke.) The water must have been thick with mines for we could see a Turkish torpedo boat, a merchantman and two tugs a long way past the Narrows and they must have been heaving mines overboard for all they were worth, and of course with a 2¼-3-knot current they soon reached us. Battleships were now drifting down with the tide as *Q.E.* took on board *Irresistible* survivors. Batteries seemed to be replying only to *Triumph* and *Ocean*, which were lying stopped still within close range.

At 6 p.m. General Recall hoisted. At 6.15 we could see a heavy list on the *Ocean*, which had been struck by a torpedo or mine, and started blowing off steam, together with *Irresistible*. At 6.28 destroyers were ordered to *Ocean* and took off her crew under heavy fire; she had a big list and began to drift down with the tide; destroyers also took off the volunteers from *Irresistible*. Both ships sank unseen later during the night in deep water.

We now fired shots at Aren Kioi village as we were drifting down with the tide, our head still pointing upstream; and at 6.50 we turned round and made for the Entrance, very nearly having a collision with the *Cornwallis* coming out!

We proceeded to Tenedos at 7.20, coming to anchor the north side at 8.43 p.m. when we found *Inflexible* in rather a bad way with a hole nearly 35 ft by 24 ft and seven collision-mats out. We sent her some of our carpenters.

We could see a big fire ablaze at Chanak after dark, also bright flashes from Turkish batteries firing at two abandoned ships.

The net result of the operations was roughly this: we had inflicted a lot of damage on the forts, but had not silenced them. They had sunk our three battleships — *Bouvet*, *Irresistible* and *Ocean* — the former with nearly all hands; *Irresistible* lost 20 or 30 only; and *Ocean* probably only a few. The French *Gaulois* had to run herself aground on Rabbit Island to avoid sinking and *Inflexible* has been badly damaged with loss of life.

Of *Agamemnon*'s damage, they scored six hits above armour and five on the armour — mostly 8-in. howitzer shells. Our capstan is completely wrecked, fore shelter deck badly damaged, two 12-pdrs damaged beyond repair, motor bollard and after funnel blown to pieces. The hit on the armour by the right gun of S 3 failed to damage the armour; only splinters causing damage. This shell flashed into our turret as it burst and one splinter drove in the inner tube of our left gun (our 12-in. guns were 'wire wound'), so it was fortunate it did not have to fire. Number 6 hit the quarterdeck by the screen door, completely wrecking it and the staghorn and blowing a big hole in the deck. All shells burst on impact into small fragments.

During the action all ships had a picket-boat away looking for mines.

At 11 p.m. 12 officers and 350 ship's company of *Ocean* were brought aboard, also some from *Irresistible*; amongst them was French Lt Millot and our snotties Donovan, Cameron, Price and Standley. Later we took on board a lot of men from *Gaulois*.

It is now thought that the tremendous shock felt by everyone in the ship was caused by the explosion of an observation mine.[2]

FRIDAY MARCH 19TH. At anchor off Tenedos. Sent away divers to *Inflexible* in order to help repair the hole in her; she had a bad list early in the morning. Everyone was awfully depressed after yesterday's battle and the Admiral sent some signals trying to cheer us up.

Signal from Admiral to Mediterranean Fleet and *Suffren*: 'Admiral regrets to announce unfortunate loss by mines of three ships,[3] which he feels was due to no lack of vigilance or forethought on the part of those concerned. We have to report very serious loss of life in *Bouvet*; but in cases of other ships it is very small. Senior officers of sub-divisions are to prepare their sub-divisions for further action with as little delay as possible, and I know that everyone will be ready to make further efforts and sacrifices when necessary. A method of overcoming mines will be found.'

ENEMY MINES: some ten days before our great assault the small Turkish minelayer Nousret *had crept down from the Narrows during darkness into Aren Kioi Bay, then believed by us to be clear of mines. Here a line of 20 mines was laid parallel to the shore, i.e. in line with our ships' advance instead of forming a barrage against it as one might have*

---

[2] An observation mine is one which can be exploded by a shore observation post.

[3] The sunken battleships today: in 1979 I learnt from Professor E. T. Hall and the Turkish diving and salvage expert, Tosun Sezen, of the present state of these ships:

Bouvet was located in position 40° 02" 30"N, 26° 17' 42"E, bottom down. Propellers in mud and still intact. Torpedo tubes removed.

Ocean in position 40° 02' 42"N, 26° 16' 33"E, bottom down. Propellers in mud, which so far has prevented the shafts from being lifted. Torpedo tubes and some other gear removed. *Irresistible* in position 40° 04' 29"N, 26° 20' 24"E. Propellers, torpedo tubes and entire engine room removed.

thought. But this was the area where the enemy had noticed that our ships had been manoeuvring and these mines in particular must have had a devastating effect on the Navy's attempt to force the Narrows on March 18th.

Yet by this time sweeping gear was already fitted to our 'Beagle'-class destroyers which enabled sweeping to be done in pairs at a speed of 10 knots against the current, but they were not used. Admiral Cunningham, writing in A Sailor's Odyssey, *states that* Scorpion *and his destroyer division spent that day (March 18th) at anchor off Tenedos.*

SEVEN: PREPARATIONS FOR LANDING MILITARY EXPEDITION

SATURDAY MARCH 20TH. At Tenedos: 'Make and Mend' in the afternoon till 5 p.m. when *Lord Nelson* and *Agamemnon* weighed and proceeded to Imbros coming to anchor on the north side at 7.15 p.m. in the devil of a gale from the south. We got orders to 'observe and annoy the enemy along the coast of Gallipoli' as our future task.

SUNDAY MARCH 21ST. 7.30 a.m. *Lord Nelson* and *Agamemnon* weighed and proceeded to the Gulf of Xeros with the object of annoying the Turks. It was a beastly day, misty and overcast, and hence we could not make out any coast at all plainly although we followed it down at about 4,000 or 5,000 yds distant. They have made me a member of the observation party, so now we are four: Mr Crookshank, Laidlaw, Symonds-Taylor and myself, and we are working 'watch and watch' during the next few days. At 5 p.m. we were off Gaba Tepe when Fluter must want to fire some 12-pdr and 9.2-in. at a barn and farmhouse and after the poor old farmer chap had run away we set his barn on fire; it was real 'baby-killing'.

At 7.15 p.m. we let go starb. anchor in north bay of Imbros in a gale; we veered to 14 shackles and backed up the brake, but the cable suddenly parted at the 2nd shackle so we have lost the starb. anchor for good as it was not buoyed and the bottom too rocky to drag for it.

MONDAY MARCH 22ND. At 7.15 arrived Port Mudros and came to single anchor near the entrance with *Lord Nelson* just ahead of us and *Queen Elizabeth* on our port beam.

The captain of marines and all marines of *Ocean* and *Irresistible* have been landed at Tenedos, the captain being made temporary governor.

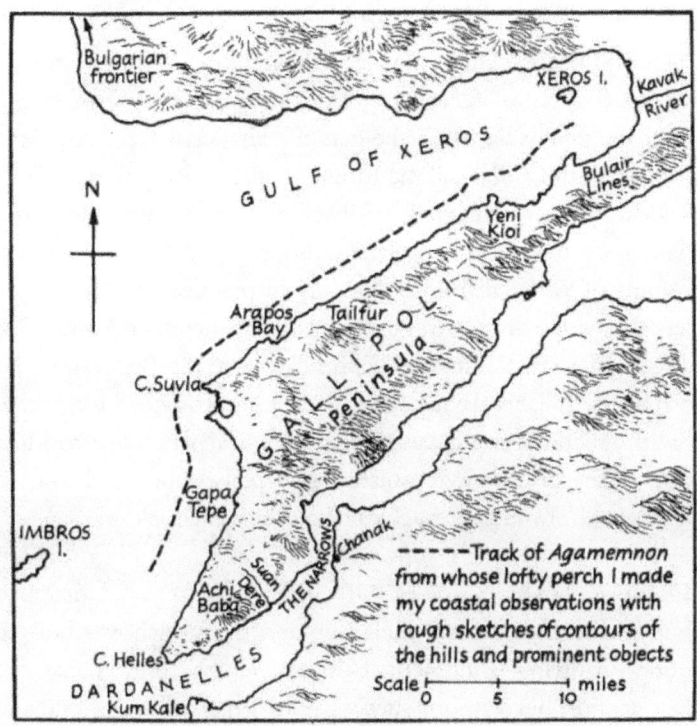

Agamemnon's reconnaissance before the landing

WEDNESDAY MARCH 24TH. At Port Mudros and Imbros. At 7 a.m. *Lord Nelson* and *Agamemnon* weighed and proceeded out of the harbour and anchored outside the bar in order to be ready to transfer 35 R.N.R. seamen from a trawler (who had 'chucked their 'ands in') and then we were to proceed to sea in order to still further annoy the Turks! Finally, we took on board Commander Douglas, observation officer and surveyor, and then weighed and proceeded to Imbros with *Lord Nelson*, coming to anchor at 6 p.m. on the south side. At 9 p.m. we again weighed in order to be off the Gallipoli coast by daylight tomorrow.

THURSDAY MARCH 25TH. Off Gallipoli. Until 9 a.m. we were laying buoys in certain positions for *Queen Elizabeth* to fire over the peninsula when she gets the chance. I went up to the foretop with Laidlaw all the forenoon and I nearly froze.

However, we managed to observe a few trenches in a bay which we noted on the chart. About 2 p.m. we fired a few rounds of 9.2-in. at Fort Sultan, also a practice shot out of the left gun of the after turret in order to test the inner A-tube. We also fired a few 9.2-in. at a windmill before the Bulair lines. At 5 p.m. we finished laying buoys and then proceeded to Imbros South Anchorage and came to anchor near where we had lost our starb. bower. We hoisted out picket-boat and started 'creeping' for the two shackles of our lost anchor-cable.

FRIDAY MARCH 26TH. Off Imbros: picket-boat dropped buoys where the 'creep' pulled up and the launch was hoisted out with diving equipment to investigate the bottom for our lost anchor, but without success. Early, the *Grampus* came and took off Commander Douglas. (He managed to make some remarkable surveys of the Gallipoli beaches.)

At 9.30 we hoisted in launch and picket-boat and then *Lord Nelson* and *Agamemnon* weighed and proceeded along the coast to the Bulair lines with the intention of destroying a building, supposed to be a magazine; but of course the Turks are not such fools as to have a magazine in such an exposed position. My afternoon in the top, and at 2 p.m. we went to Gen.

Quarters and opened fire with the fore turret full charge, which shook the top like blazes as well as making a d—d awful row. We went on firing until 4 p.m., altogether 44 rounds at the fort getting a few direct hits and remainder just short in a trench making huge splashes of earth, etc., smothering the building. *Lord Nelson* also fired, but very poorly; *Charlemagne* and *Askold* were firing at trenches and earthworks.

At 4 p.m. we proceeded back to Imbros and came to single anchor at 8.15 p.m. in South Bay while *Lord Nelson* left for Port Mudros with our mail. German aeroplane was reported over Gallipoli this morning.

SUNDAY MARCH 28TH. Off Gallipoli and Bulair: weighed at 9 a.m. and proceeded with *Lord Nelson* to Suvla Point and keeping 2 miles off the coast steamed right down to Bulair as far as we could go up the Gulf of Xeros. We again saw all the trenches and earthworks up the slopes to Bulair village and a lot of cattle.

In the forenoon got an urgent W/T signal from V.A. stating ships at Tenedos were being attacked by two German aeroplanes, which dropped bombs trying to hit *Ark Royal*; one bomb falling 100 yds ahead of her and another 10 yds off her bow. At 2 p.m. Worsley reported sighting three enemy aeroplanes coming over Gallipoli towards us and so we closed up anti-aircraft guns, but later we concluded that owing to their flapping wings they must be eagles — hence the excitement ended.

All the villages about Bulair at the end of the Gulf were absolutely burnt out and destroyed by the French squadron previously. I was up in the foretop and saw a few horsemen galloping away when they saw us. We sighted many floating objects for which we altered course to avoid in case they should be mines. The water up there is very clear and it was a beautiful day and no wind at all. Steaming back at 3.15 p.m. we sighted smoke from ships in the Straits, but it was difficult to tell whether it was the *Goeben* or a tug or what; anyhow Fluter reported it and increased speed to 12 knots evidently thinking he was going to meet the Turkish fleet. However, at 6.30 p.m. we arrived at North Anchorage, Imbros, and found the French ships *Henri IV* and *Charlemagne* still there, also *Talbot* and a couple of French destroyers. During the day *Queen Elizabeth* bombarded the Narrows' forts from a position off Gaba Tepe.

Signal from Malta to Admiral: 'I am preparing 26 lighters with bullet-proof iron shelters to send you for landing troops and horses. I have been told to have them at Mudros by April 4th.'

MONDAY MARCH 29TH. Off Gallipoli: 7 a.m. weighed and proceeded past Suvla Point along the coast towards Bulair in order to support destroyer *Mosquito* with Commander Douglas on board her. *Mosquito* was proceeding down the coast accompanied by cruiser *Talbot* which fired at farmhouses in some of the coves. All these bays, houses, etc., have been closely observed by us during the last week, but *Talbot*, being new at the job, probably takes advantage of firing an angry shot at a deserted farmhouse. It was a beastly day, raining hard all the forenoon, eventually obscuring the land from us completely. We stopped engines at 11 a.m., when off the windmills, and proceeded again at noon in order to support *Mosquito* off Gaba Tepe.

We were off Gaba Tepe at 4 p.m. Weather had quite cleared up and turned out a jolly afternoon. I went up to the crow's-nest in order to try and observe any howitzers over the ridge, but I failed to see anything in the nature of a howitzer nor yet any sign of life.

On March 29th I decoded the following signal: 'Immediate steps to be taken to provide at earliest possible moment protection of battleships against submarine mines in Dardanelles by means of rectangular framework suspended from lighters extending 30 ft under water. Framework to carry light wire netting. A pair of 100-ton lighters to be placed each side of ship as far forward as possible.'

Perhaps a desperate last resort, but this impractical device came to nothing as far as I know.

Also a signal referring to the construction of bullet-proof lighters for landing troops and 'smoke lighters' for screening troops. 'Six lighters are also being constructed for mine catching, one on either side of a ship', but I do not at present see how it should work.

TUESDAY MARCH 30TH. Arrived Port Mudros at 7 a.m.; collier *Barrington Court* came alongside at 8 a.m. and we began taking in 533 tons which was not completed till 12.30 p.m., partly owing to having to 'break bulk' in No. 1 hold which was all battened down for sea. In the harbour were most of the French ships, also *Askold*, *Inflexible*, with about 8° list to port, *Queen Elizabeth*, *Cornwallis*, *Swiftsure*, *Triumph*, *Prince George*, but not many transports, probably because a big military camp on the beach has accommodated the soldiers. *Barrington Court* had aboard her six old service cutters strengthened up to be used for a pontoon landing bridge.

At 4 p.m. we took aboard five bodies from *Inflexible* and proceeded to sea at 5 p.m. in order to bury the dead. One of the poor devils was an R.C. so we took aboard with us an R.C.

parson to bury him. There was a nasty lop outside and at 6.30 p.m. we stopped both engines and committed the five bodies to the deep. At 7 p.m. we again proceeded and came to anchor north Imbros at 12.15 a.m.

WEDNESDAY MARCH 31ST. Off north coast, Gulf of Xeros: weighed at 9 a.m. and proceeded towards the Turkish/Bulgarian frontier and very nearly caused a Balkan war by Fluter wanting to fire on a railway bridge which *he* thought was Turkish, but, of course, it was really Bulgarian. However, we then proceeded down the coast into the Gulf and hugged the coast to the north for the benefit of observation purposes. I was in the foretop all afternoon and kept my eyes glued on the coast all the time, but not any sign of earthworks, guns, trenches, etc., was seen. It appeared to be a most fertile and pretty country with a large number of cattle grazing; also a few scattered little houses besides farmhouses and small villages. We sighted the French ship *Henri IV*, and *Talbot* right up the Gulf near Xeros Islet. A little before this we passed a small cove which contained a few sheds, houses, etc., all destroyed; beside this was a locomotive boiler and a sunken barge. It looked to have been quite an industrial little place before the Frenchman came along and knocked it all down.

Passing Xeros Islet we saw a boat with three men in it. Later, when we again returned to the islet, we sent away a cutter armed, and with handcuffs, in order to make prisoners the three wretched men in the boat whom Fluter thought were Turks. The cutter also took with her a candle lamp to be put on top of the island in order to annoy the Turks. (The light could not be seen even through a Ross telescope one mile away!) It was really very comic watching the cutter's crew marching about with rifles to the top of the rock where they stuck up the light. How the Turks must have laughed! Then we hoisted out the launch, picket-boat and 1st cutter, which were to be towed in by the picket-boat with dummies close to Bulair in order to try and draw the enemy's fire and so discover if the trenches were occupied. Firstly the proper crews pulled the boats round the ship to show them to the Turks — all except the 1st cutter, which started to sink and so was hoisted in again! The launch was then filled up with dummies after berthing on our seaward side which the Turks could not see. We then proceeded across to the other side of Gulf close to Bulair followed by the picket-boat towing 2nd cutter and the 'prize'. This contained three Greeks, in a starving condition, who had been marooned on the deserted islet, owing to the Turks firing at them and wrecking their mast so that they could not sail back to Imbros, about 40 miles away. At 7 p.m. amid great interest from the ship's company the 'prize' came alongside and three fine old Greeks came aboard, very politely taking off their caps in doing so. In spite of the fact they were unarmed they were fallen in under a guard and searched, which they thought really humorous. Then the parson came along and, judging from their expressions, the Greeks thought he was at least 'Lord High Executioner'! The Greeks were then taken by the wardroom mess-man (who knew a little Greek) to his abode, passing through a gaping and bewildered crowd of ship's company who thought at least the victims should be strung up at the yardarm.

Meanwhile Worsley in the picket-boat towed the launch and cutter towards the shore, returning at 8.15 p.m., not having been fired on although it was a bright moonlit night. We then hoisted in our boats and some us couldn't resist a rag with the dummies. Here I was observed by the Rabbit and in trouble again, accused of behaving 'like a d—d ordinary seaman'.

Eventually at 9.45 p.m. we proceeded at 6 knots so as to reach Imbros by the morning, and there set free our Greek heroes and their boat, which we had brought with us on board.

THURSDAY APRIL 1ST. Off Gallipoli: weighed at 9.30 a.m. and proceeded with *Lord Nelson* towards Gaba Tepe to within 3,000 yds of shore and then to Cape Helles where there were various destroyers, sweepers and *Albion* and *Canopus*; *Albion* firing at a battery near Kum Kale. We were getting in the danger area of mines so turned 16 points, passed Suvla Point and proceeded to Arapos Bay where at 3.30 p.m. we fired about 62 rounds of 12-pdr at a rotten little brushwood hut which we failed to demolish; meanwhile the *Lord Nelson* fired a few rounds at some trenches. Between the trenches and the hut were five camels which continued to graze absolutely unperturbed by our bursting shells; Fluter actually did *not* want to fire on the beasts!

At 5.30 p.m. we were again off Gaba Tepe and as the sun set we got out boats and did the same funny landing feint, by coming in close to the shore and throwing dummies in the boat so that the Turks could not help seeing them. As we were close in and only a couple of thousand yds from one of their howitzers, we went to Gen. Quarters while the picket-boat towed the launch and 2nd cutter towards the shore firing a Maxim to try and draw the enemy's fire, but without success. They returned at 7.15 and were hoisted in. We then proceeded to Imbros coming to anchor at 8.30 p.m. at usual North Anchorage.

W/T signal from *Talbot* stating they have picked up Turkish refugee — an engineer corporal in a Turkish regiment who has given very useful and reliable information stating that troops are quartered at Yeni Kioi village and various other places.

(This was evidently the bloke we saw on the beach on Monday waving his arms. We then thought it was Commander Douglas doing some surveying as is often the case with him to land and make sketches. If Fluter had taken any notice when it was reported to him, we might have made the capture instead of *Talbot*.)

Everyone is absolutely fed up with this show and have been for the past week; it is getting too boring for words.

FRIDAY APRIL 2ND. Off Gallipoli: weighed at 9 a.m. in order to go and annoy the Turks (or let them annoy us) together with *Lord Nelson*. We cannot even have a rest on Good Friday and we must turn it into a day of 'frightfulness' instead of having a decent rest for a change. We went to Suvla and then to Cape Helles where we turned 16 points and patrolled the coast as far as Arapos and thence back to Gaba Tepe. Finally, we packed up at 6 p.m. and proceeded to Imbros, coming to East Anchorage at 7.15 p.m.

W/T signal stating that *Albion* and *Canopus* have been attacked by aeroplanes, but the bombs did not hit them. It is also reported that two Turkish destroyers of the 'Sultan Hisar'-class have escaped during the night out of the Straits and probably gone to Smyrna.

SATURDAY APRIL 3RD. Weighed at 7.45 and proceeded at 12 knots past Suvla Point down the south side of Gulf. Turned 16 points when off Yeni Kioi windmills and patrolled along the coast as far as Cape Helles. Fluter then saw a steamer near Imbros which we chased and found her name and reported her to the Admiral as flying French colours together with her description. We then went on to Imbros and at 5 p.m. came to anchor on the south-east side. After Quarters at 4.15 p.m. we carried out the evolution of 'Preparing to tow aft', much to the disgust of the ship's company as it was their proper Make and Mend, and naturally they had a moan about it.

W/T signal stating that Commander Sampson wants two midshipmen of light weight and of good signal knowledge for observation purposes. Of course I sent my name in, being over 10 stone and of course having an excellent knowledge of signals (?), but unfortunately Fluter told me I was too heavy; also Pearson.

SUNDAY APRIL 4TH. Off Gallipoli and at Mudros: Easter Sunday and yet we must go and be annoyed by the Turks. We weighed at 7.45 a.m. and first chased a Greek steamer for a time until we were certain of her identity. We then went to Gaba Tepe and proceeded at 6 knots to Cape Helles to waste time till being relieved by *Lord Nelson*, which left Port Mudros at 9 a.m. Near the Entrance and just inside were many minesweepers supported by destroyers, while *Prince of Wales* and *London* were in the Entrance firing at batteries on both sides which were replying by firing at these ships and at the minesweepers. The old *London* got hit by a 6-in. howitzer.

We arrived Mudros and came to anchor at 5.15 p.m.; I went away in the sea-boat to *Q.E.* We got a mail and a good lot of parcels but, of course, my photographic gear did not turn up; I got two letters. Strong northerly gale blowing.

MONDAY APRIL 5TH. Owing to the bad weather and gale we waited till 2 p.m., when collier *Amicus* weighed and after dropping many anchors, which all dragged, she got alongside. We had 370 tons to take in and it poured with rain all day and put everyone in the worst of tempers.

W/T signal stating that all the troops and landing equipment are to be ready by the 12th inst., so it looks as if they will be landing fairly soon, though the transports are at present at Alexandria.

TUESDAY APRIL 6TH. At Port Mudros: a beastly wet day and my forenoon watch with Mr Hammet. During the forenoon a tug towing one lighter arrived, she having lost a lot more in her tow during the heavy weather.

In the afternoon, I went on the beach with Anderson, and we walked in the pouring rain over to the town of Mudros. On the way we went through a camp of French African troops, Senegalese, absolutely black, but fine, big and well-built men who often saluted us; they had French officers. At the village we purchased chocolate, oranges, Turkish Delight, etc. and got quite pally with one old Greek who had travelled about a good deal to England, America, etc.

At 5.30 p.m. *Talbot* sailed in order to accompany the damaged *Inflexible* to Malta with *Canopus*. We were to escort her originally, but now *Agamemnon* and *Lord Nelson*, as well as two old ships, are earmarked to go right through to the Sea of Marmara and thus threaten Constantinople.

At 6.30 p.m. *Inflexible* weighed and proceeded out of harbour 'manning ship', while all ships did likewise and cheered her as she went out. She was certainly a fine sight and looked as though nothing much was wrong with her except for the foretop roof being smashed in; nevertheless her outward appearance was deceptive for she was in a very dangerous condition in spite of the efforts of the chief constructor who has fitted a flexible metal pad. (Constructor was telegraphed for immediately after the disaster and had a special train to Marseilles and then a French T.B. brought him at full speed out here.) *Inflexible* had on her decks baulks of timber and life-saving apparatus in case she should founder during the voyage to Malta. *Canopus* sailed just after her and later we learnt she had to tow *Inflexible* stern first much of the way until nearly reaching Malta. *Inflexible* then proudly entered Grand Harbour under her own power.

WEDNESDAY APRIL 7TH. At Port Mudros and at sea: a beautiful day. Sent in a recreation party during the forenoon. I ran the cutter, but unfortunately got lurked for pistol drill as some silly ass could not use one the other day at Xeros. In the afternoon I landed with the other blokes for a paperchase and after running for half an hour over various rocky hills, I came down and badly sprained my ankle. We then made our way back to the beach and found the Blue Peter hoisted — the first time since Portland five or six months ago.

When we got on board we weighed and proceeded out of harbour at 10 knots in order to look for a lot of lost lighters which carried away recently during gales while being towed in the Doro Channel. At 7.30 p.m. we got a signal stating the lighters had been found, but it was too late to get back so we stayed at sea.

THURSDAY APRIL 8TH. My Middle with Mr Hammet and I caused the ship to go back in order to communicate with a tug and so got poor old Hammet in the rattle; anyhow I woke up old Fluter three or four times! A beautiful day. We went to Gen. Quarters during the forenoon. At 8.30 a.m. when south of Skyros we turned 16 points and headed for Mudros, arriving at 5.30 p.m. We tested our hand-steering gear on passage but could not keep within a point of our course.

Back at Mudros, at 7 p.m. steamer *King John* came alongside to remove our smashed hydraulic engine for repair at Malta and then *Riverside* with ammunition: 634 12-pdr, 37 9.2-in. all 'common shell' and 41 12-in., she not having nearly enough for our requirements.

FRIDAY APRIL 9TH. Weighed at 7 a.m. and proceeded to Cape Helles to relieve *Lord Nelson*. We then steamed down the coast stopping as usual to examine Gaba Tepe and Suvla Bay. When we got to Arapos Bay we saw some soldiers running out of a house and so started blazing away with 12-pdrs, also a couple of rounds of 9.2-in., the first one completely demolishing a house. During the forenoon we had revolver practice as a towed target. I shot all right with my right hand, but not so well with my left.

We steamed back to Imbros coming to North Anchorage at 7.30 p.m.

SATURDAY APRIL 10TH. Weighed at 7.30 a.m. and proceeded towards Bulgarian coast.

At 10.30 a.m. we sighted a Greek steamer, which we chased, and after firing a few rounds of blank 12-pdr she hove to; when near enough we lowered the cutter with Mr Holmes, Greenway, Mr Dale and myself all armed with revolvers for the coming fray. When we got alongside her the boarding party got out and examined her while I had to stay in the cutter: meanwhile the Greeks simply hurled oranges into our boat for all they were worth, each bloke having caught about 40 oranges. After 20 minutes we decided she was filled up only with oranges from Jaffa, so we let her go and then proceeded until the Bulgarian town of Dede Aghatch was in sight; we then turned 16 points and eventually steamed up the north side of the Gulf of Xeros.

The only other excitement was when passing 2 miles to seaward of Cape Grimea the leadsman got soundings of only 7 fathoms — an uncharted shoal, but alarming at the time.

We stopped twice to fire at small houses where we saw soldiers; regretfully we wounded some unfortunate cattle in knocking down the house. We fired at the same old cove with a boiler, barges, etc; the latter we sank and eventually set the place ablaze. We then proceeded along the coast and fired about 50 rounds of 12-pdrs over the hill into Yeni Kioi village. Just before this, however, we picked up a Greek in a boat who had had both his companions shot by the Turks. We then proceeded to Imbros arriving North Anchorage at 9.30 p.m.

SUNDAY APRIL 11TH. Weighed at 9 a.m. and started once more on the same old round of horror. Proceeded up the Gulf to Bulair in order to shell that village and so destroy more women, children and other peaceful citizens, who had not already evacuated the village. We fired 12-pdrs at a mosque, or rather at a building, but of course most of them hit the mosque and churchyard, much to the delight of Fluter, who put on a broad smile. We then let off a 12-pdr broadside at Yeni Kioi village and steamed back to our usual North Anchorage, Imbros, arriving at 7 p.m. We immediately got out our nets as Fluter now realises there is quite a good possibility of torpedo attack, our being in sight of the enemy coast.

Signal from the Admiral: 'Ships are warned against a spy, Caputo, who is trying to find employment in the fleet. His distinguishing feature is a scar on his face.' We often had a good laugh!

MONDAY APRIL 12TH. At anchor, Imbros: tried to furl our nets at 5.30 a.m. but, through breaking a winch, could not brail up so we weighed and proceeded to Gulf of Xeros with our nets out. At 8 a.m. stopped both engines; I went away in the cutter to *Ark Royal* for orders, and while waiting had a yarn with most of their officers and a good look round the ship. More than half the ship is given to aeroplanes alone; they have now got seven machines and another one to come; their fastest machine can do 105 m.p.h. They have a big 'Wright' machine amongst them and a machine which had previously raided Heligoland.

During the forenoon we continued to steam with our nets out and got barely 6 knots out of the ship. At 3 p.m. *Ark Royal* sent up a seaplane, which started spotting for us, while we fired half-charge 9.2-in. over the hill into Tailfur village by indirect fire as we could not see our target at all, not even from the foretop or crow's-nest. We fired 18 rounds altogether — trying to drop them on the magazine. Finally we packed up and came to anchor north of Imbros after meeting *Lord Nelson*.

TUESDAY APRIL 13TH. To Dede Aghatch, Bulgaria: we got orders from the Admiral to go to Dede Aghatch to bring off an English colonel who is said to be on a diplomatic mission. Weighed at 7 a.m. with *Lord Nelson* and proceeded down Gallipoli coast past Arapos Bay with all guns at the 'Ready' and proceeded as far as Yeni Sheir where we turned round leaving *Lord Nelson*, and proceeded on a northerly course to Dede Aghatch, where we came to anchor in the roadstead at 3.30 p.m. A national salute of 21 guns was fired and the Bulgarian ensign was 'broken at the fore'. It was a pouring wet day and very misty and everything on land had a dismal aspect.

The town ran right along the shore, there being a conspicuous lighthouse and mosque also a small harbour for the local fishing boats (mostly lateen rig and caiques). There were in the roadstead about a dozen small steamers, mostly Italian, belonging to the factory company on the beach. A small customs boat put out to us: we sent in our picket-boat with Fluter, etc., to see the Consul. The colonel did not turn up. It came on to blow from the south later; the steamers weighed and put to sea, returning when it abated somewhat.

WEDNESDAY APRIL 14TH. A beautiful day and the wind has dropped. I went away in the cutter at 9 a.m. in tow of the picket-boat to the harbour. We then pulled in to the shallow little quay and about an hour later Greenway and Berthon brought along four or five Bulgars and the British, French and Italian Consuls. The Bulgars were the Commandant, Senior Naval Officer, Préfet, Sous-Préfet, all fat creatures dressed up in gorgeous uniforms; we had to bring them out to the picket-boat. Then we had a most comic incident: both boats were rolling to a heavy swell and, by bad judgement, I brought the cutter somewhere amidships of the picket-boat, so the old Commandant jumped out, knocked his head on the funnel and then walked aft hanging on for dear life to the screen all covered with wet paint with six men trying to pull him off. Coming back to the ship the old fatty — the Sous-Préfet — laughed at me in the cutter getting wet, but when we got to the ship he was so seasick that he could not get aboard and I had to take him back. After many exertions, all the others, helped by proddings from the bowman's boathook, climbed up the makeshift ladder, our accommodation ladder having been shot away. After looking very bewildered they found their way to Fluter amid the melodious strains of the Bulgarian ragtime anthem, while the Guard presented arms. After this proceeding one of the Bulgars was so nervous that he sat on the wet paint on the capstan. They were then shown over the after turret and all the marvels in the working of a modern 12-in. gun; then they went round the ship. At 2 p.m. the Bulgars left with the usual ceremony and, when passing the sternwalk, gave Fluter a cheer; salutes were then fired, 13 guns for the Commandant, nine for Senior Naval Officer and seven for Vice-Consul.

We weighed and proceeded out of the 3-mile limit and anchored at 2.40 again. I went away in the picket-boat at 6.30 p.m. and after a rough passage we brought off Colonel Napier and Mr Fitzmaurice, the latter supposed to be the most influential man in Bulgaria.

At 9 p.m. we weighed and proceeded towards Lemnos so as to make Mudros at dawn.

THURSDAY APRIL 15TH. At 6.15 arrived Port Mudros. What a change! The harbour is now absolutely full of transports and ships of all kinds: there are said to be about 150,000 troops here ready to land now, apart from some of the Naval Division. I then went to the flagship with reports in the picket-boat.

At 11.15 collier *Penmorvak* came alongside and we began coaling, taking in 720 tons, having intervals for lunch and tea; we finally finished at 6.15 p.m. after a hard day's work.

During the afternoon four or five more big transports came in, mostly Australian troops. There are just less than 100 big ships in here now.

FRIDAY APRIL 16TH. Supply ship *Swanly* and ammunition ship *Tristram* came alongside at 7 a.m. and we started taking in stores and ammunition at once: eight rounds of 12-in. and 45 rounds of 9.2-in. (T.N.T.). A number of transports left in the morning for Skyros; also some more arrived.

At 11 a.m. got urgent signal *en clair* from transport *Manitou*: 'S.O.S. Have been torpedoed in 38° 50'N, 25°E by German.' Destroyers went out to her assistance and later made a report on what had happened. It appears that a Turkish torpedo boat suddenly appeared round the point south of Skyros without colours, approached the transport and after hoisting Turkish colours gave her 10 minutes to clear. Thereupon there was a tremendous panic, boats were crowded and men started jumping in the sea, so that they lost about 60 men. The T.B. then closed *Manitou* to 100 yds and fired three small torpedoes, all of which missed the ship. She then made off at full speed for Smyrna but according to a later signal was cut off: 'Turkish torpedo-boat, chased by destroyers *Jed* and *Kennet*, was cut off by *Minerva* and *Wear* in Khios Straits. She beached herself in Kalamuti Bay. Troops again got aboard *Manitou* and later she proceeded to Port Mudros.'

In the afternoon we had a fine picnic with Fluter and after rounders and a bathe we had a decent tea partly provided by Fluter.

Tonight the *E 15*, *E 14* and *B 6* left for the Dardanelles and proceeded upstream hoping to torpedo a Turkish warship in Kilia Liman Bay.

SATURDAY APRIL 17TH. French cruiser *Julien de Gravière* and the unhappy transport *Manitou* arrived early.

Several urgent signals about submarine *E 15*, which, unfortunately, has run aground about 300 yds off Kephez Point. An aeroplane has been ordered to go up and drop bombs on any boats that may be seen near the submarine and should the Turks be seen capturing the submarine, bombs are to be dropped on it. At 4 p.m. we sent away Mr Price and several hands who are to take part in the landing of troops. Several of our signalmen are also going to land.

At 2 p.m. most of the gunroom landed for a paperchase, Pearson and Anderson being the hares; about 15 miles over rocky country. Arrived at 6 p.m. absolutely dead-beat just in time to get the boat back.

Submarine *E 14* returned, having reported *E 15* aground near Kephez Point; *B 6* has not yet returned.

SUNDAY APRIL 18TH. Our first Sunday in port for ever so long and quite a treat to have this three-day rest and enjoyment. After church the band of the 5th Australian Infantry came aboard and gave us a very good patriotic show of music, also the Scots gave a display of pipes and dancing. They were very popular with the ship's company and spent an enjoyable day aboard, not departing before 6 p.m. In the afternoon most of the officers landed for another picnic, but I could not go and so wrote letters and developed six plates. At 6.30 p.m. we weighed and proceeded to Tenedos to relieve Admiral Nicholson arriving North Anchorage 11 p.m. Took on Senior Officer which delights Fluter greatly! Tonight the picket-boats of *Triumph* and *Majestic* went into the Straits to torpedo *E 15*; *Triumph*'s boat failed in her attack, but *Majestic*'s succeeded, afterwards being sunk by gunfire. Her crew were saved by the other boat.

MONDAY APRIL 19TH. At Dardanelles: weighed at 10 p.m. and proceeded with our 1st picket-boat in tow (fitted with dropping gear) in order to torpedo *E 15* tonight. Lay off the entrance until 3 p.m. when we slipped the picket-boat and proceeded inside to Morto Bay in order to get a view of the submarine. Before entering at 11 a.m. we met Lt-Comdr Brodie in *B 6* who informed us he had been alongside *E 15* which had heeled over more than 90° and so has been damaged severely inside and hence is unserviceable: apparently all the crew must have been lost. (Later we heard that many were saved.)

We closed up at Gen. Quarters and they fired a few 'small stuff' at us as well as a couple of decent howitzer shells (about 6-in.). We saw our submarine *E 15* or rather part of her conning tower, which contradicts *B 6*'s statement about her being nearly capsized.

We then came out of the Straits, picked up picket-boat and proceeded to Tenedos where Fluter, being S.N.O., hoisted 'O-TN' (optional-hands to bathe) and most ships' companies bathed. I then had to hunt the island with Fluter and land him in a cutter to go on to the aerodrome. Got out net defence later.

TUESDAY APRIL 20TH. At Tenedos: my day for picket-boat. A northerly gale got up making it uncomfortably rough, so that I got soaked every trip. At 11.30 a.m. having hoisted in the picket-boat, we weighed and proceeded to the South Anchorage owing to the weather. After tea I had to take Fluter again to see the aerodrome; from later information I gathered they have 25 machines there and were attacked the other day by Taubes, one bomb falling 20 ft off the shed. I then had to go to the *Ribble* for secret letters and nearly got run down once or twice as no one had lights. Sub-Lieutenants Greenway, Laidlaw, Berthon and Walker have all been appointed to destroyers out here, so we had Guest Night and about six wardroom officers dined with us.

Turkey reports the capture of three officers and 21 men, being the crew of *E 15*; amongst them is the ex-British Vice-Consul. We hear now that they had on board a month's provisions and were going through to the Sea of Marmara.

WEDNESDAY APRIL 21ST. Had to turn out at 5.30 to furl nets and at 7 a.m. collier *Ingleside* came alongside and we began taking in 232 tons which was finished at 9.10 a.m. in pouring rain. In the afternoon *Swansea Vale* came alongside and we began ammunitioning, taking in 273 9.2-in. shells and cartridges and 240 12-pdr.

At 5 p.m. we weighed and, preceded by *Lord Nelson*, went to relieve the ships guarding the Entrance of the Straits. Hoisted out picket-boat and sent her away for the night with Bowes-Lyon and Berthon to patrol the coast near Yeni Sheir.

THURSDAY APRIL 22ND. Off the Dardanelles: still hanging about the Entrance. Our aeroplanes were to have made a raid on Maidos, a town beyond the Narrows, but high wind prevented it. During the forenoon cruiser *Sapphire* made dashes in the Entrance trying to lay buoys for the future transport anchorage after the Landing, but she was under fire of a few howitzers. During the day she laid only three buoys; I tried to get a photo of her under fire, but the wind always blew the splashes away too quickly.

We patrolled the coast to Gaba Tepe and watched 50 Turks marching along the road evidently relieving some other men; anyhow we loaded S 2 and S 3 with shrapnel, and had it not been for an L.T.O. (torpedo rating) switching on a searchlight too soon, we might have killed a few Turks.

Patrolled near the Entrance during the night.

FRIDAY APRIL 23RD. Still off the Entrance patrolling with *Lord Nelson*. Went to Gen. Quarters during the forenoon to test communications.

W/T signal stating that 'operations are definitely taking place on Sunday', i.e. the landing of troops. We are to cover minesweeping destroyers and *Lynn*, which is going to lay out a net inside the Straits. We are to be known as the 5th Squadron under command of Fluter. We have now a number of Channel steamers fitted as sweepers, e.g. *Lynx*, *Roebuck*, etc. — Weymouth boats, but they don't appear to be in use.

At 2 p.m. we saw two of our aeroplanes flying to Maidos; they were fired on by shrapnel several times but not hit; later we heard the reports of the bombs and gunfire. At 5.20 p.m. we were relieved by *Vengeance* and *Prince George* and proceeded to north Tenedos with *Lord Nelson*. Several transports have come down here with lighters and more are coming tomorrow.

SATURDAY APRIL 24TH. The eve of great events. We took in 120 tons of coal early in the forenoon from *Cairngowan*. In the Dog Watches *Swanly* came alongside and we started taking in various stores; three destroyers then came alongside us for stores.

Sent away both picket-boats, one with S. Taylor for *Euryalus*, and the other with Banks to *Cornwallis*. Then a signal came, saying they wanted a midshipman for beach party at 'V' Beach (*River Clyde*) and I stood by quite thrilled with six-shooter, etc., ready to go; but, alas, the job fell through, being cancelled by a later signal.

Several transports came round during the night. Landing conditions, which are now reported every few hours, seem very favourable for a successful landing tomorrow.

EIGHT: LANDINGS ON GALLIPOLI

SUNDAY APRIL 25TH. Landing of the Allied Army in Gallipoli: *'Der Tag'*. Turned out at ¼ to 4 to find we were steaming towards the Entrance of the Dardanelles. Accordingly after having a little breakfast, I collected my camera, notebook and telescope, and proceeded up to the maintop just as dawn appeared. We had cleared for immediate action previously, having gone to Action Stations at 4.30 a.m. At 4.50 ships started firing on Gaba Tepe, and at 5 a.m. the general bombardment was begun by all ships except us.

At 5.15 it was quite light and many ships were following a long way astern of us: transports, trawlers full of troops, picket-boats towing cutters also full of troops, and lighters all ready for landing.

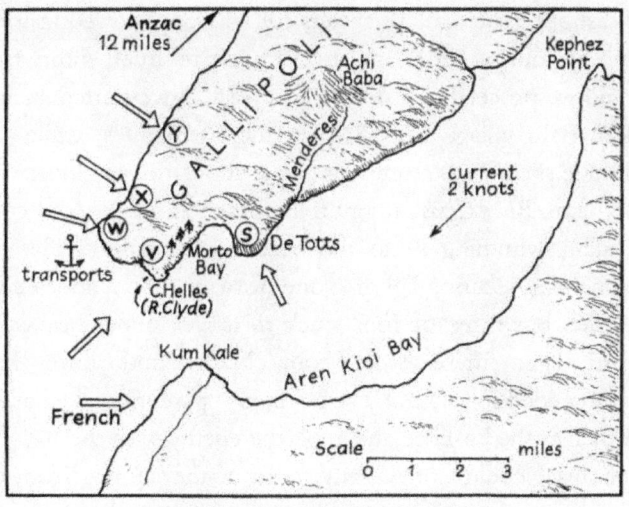

Allied landings, April 25th 1915

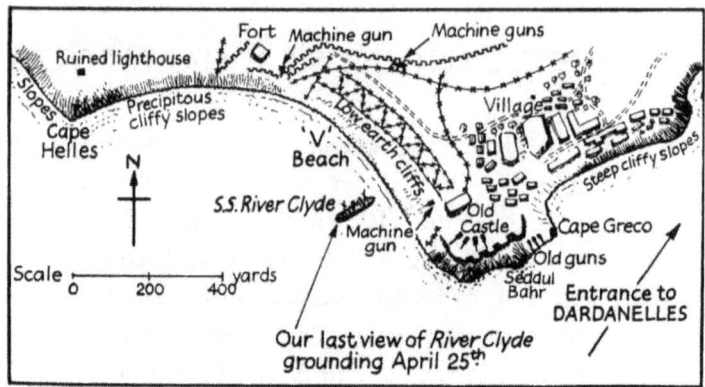

Detail from one of Cmdr Douglas's surveys of Seddul Bahr coast

Collier *River Clyde* following in our wake was painted to match the cliffs at Seddul Bahr and had lighters lashed alongside her and gangplanks running along the ship's side; everything ready for running her up on the beach and making a rush ashore. At 6 a.m. 12 cutters full of troops towed in to 'X' Beach by four picket-boats; at 6.15 boats returned empty from 'X' and we proceeded inside Straits. At 6.25 we started shelling Seddul Bahr village with 12-pdrs for 10 minutes, while they had three shots at us from Kum Kale about 100 yds short.

At 7 a.m. *River Clyde* ran upon the beach at full speed; I could see men swimming in to the beach under heavy rifle- and shrapnel-fire securing lighters; one or two of them appeared to get killed but three or four stuck to it well under heavy fire. (Heard later these were four N.O.s and have been recommended for V.C.s.) The soldiers apparently waited a little and then rushed ashore and took the enemy with the bayonet. After this I could not see any more of the landing from our position outside the Straits.

At 7.30 four trawlers (each holding 250 men) with life-boats proceeded past Morto Bay and landed unopposed at the foot of the very steep cliff under De Totts battery. They disembarked almost leisurely and climbed up to the top where they dug themselves in. We learnt that they met a few Turks hiding on the way and reported having lost three officers and seven men, but captured one sergeant and six soldiers.

At 8.30 a.m. we dropped back off Seddul Bahr and saw the *Queen Elizabeth* firing 15-in. shell into Seddul Bahr at about 3,000 or 4,000 yds range. All this time a heavy musketry fire had been going on at all beaches except 'U' (the K.O.S.B. were at 'Y' and Australians at 'Z'). At 8.50 our after turret opened fire on battery at Kum Kale. Proceeded up Straits again to find *Asiatic* disappearing, guns still firing. Owing to funnel smoke I went down to the after turret and pinched some breakfast from Mr Gardner. At 9 a.m. general bombardment slackens; quite a relief to the incessant roar of heavy guns going on since 5 a.m.

At 9.15 the kite balloon in sight off the east coast, being secured to steamer. The French troops landing in fine style at Kum Kale without much resistance; field-guns dropping shells on Fort 6 near Frenchmen.

The whole setting was most dramatic. We were conscious of a mighty armada — setting forth to conquer the Dardanelles, to open the way to Constantinople, and perhaps end the war.

At 9.30 steamer *Lynn* moored the anti-mining net (about ½ a mile) just above De Totts battery, but a little later the net began to sag and, finally, at 11 a.m. it carried right away and drifted down with the current.

At 10.40 we did a run-up with destroyers (six 'Beagle'-class), sweeping a passage in the middle of the Straits; got fired at by big stuff 100 yds short of us; we retaliated, firing S 3 at mobile guns on Asiatic side — impossible to locate with accuracy over the ridge.

Vengeance by herself, anchored in bay above 'U' landing, firing hard all day at Achi Baba and getting straddled frequently by big stuff. At 12.30 one of our aeroplanes passed over us. (1.30p.m. I came down and got some more food in the after turret.) Our soldiers now cutting wire on top of Seddul Bahr and forming a proper line; army signal station in place of lighthouse.

At 2.15 did another run-up with destroyers sweeping as far as Domuz Deresi and got fired on about six or seven times by 8-in. howitzers, all of which burst on striking the water. 3 p.m. *Queen Elizabeth* firing salvoes into Seddul Bahr, and we can see our soldiers on top, entrenched and making dashes at cutting wire entanglements.

At 5.30 did another run-up with destroyers and got fired at again, one going 20 yds over, another 100 yds short. We saw a minelayer and couple of T.B.s, patrolling above Chanak, and a warship. Our destroyers now fired on heavily by shrapnel from field-guns at Aren Kioi; *Mosquito* being hit, her First Lieutenant killed and 20 wounded.

At 5 p.m. I watched Frenchmen landing horses, guns, etc., at Kum Kale; aeroplane being fired on heavily by Maxim and shrapnel. Lying close off Morto Bay, near cliff, we were surprised to hear rifle bullets whistling over our heads and found that they were sniping at us from shore.

There was now a big fleet of transports anchored off Seddul Bahr out of the danger area, the main channel being left clear; roughly 50 ships off Seddul Bahr and nearly as many off Gaba Tepe. 6 p.m. More heavy musketry-fire at Seddul Bahr. 6.15 Heavy shrapnel-fire on French boats landing at Kum Kale.

At 6.35 another run-up with destroyers; we put a couple of rounds into Aren Kioi. Our usual howitzer friends on European side potted at us again from Suan Dere; one whizzed past the main top only a foot or two clear and I could actually see, and almost feel, the fellow as he shot past and fell harmlessly in the ditch 20 yds clear of the ship.

At 7.40 sounded 'Cease Fire'; proceeded out of Straits to patrol off 'Y' Beach for the night; saw a decent fire burning in Seddul Bahr village, now in our occupation. We were at Action Stations nearly 15 hours and all food, etc., was taken with us.

The K.O.S.B., who had landed at 'Y' Beach, first of all advanced some miles and then had to retire suffering many casualties. They were sending urgent signals for ammunition during the night and later, after some confusion, 'Y' Beach had to be evacuated with a certain amount of gear left behind. There was, however, some criticism of the support afforded by *Goliath*.

Other events today: the Australian submarine *AE 2* (Lt-Comdr Stoker) went up the Straits with a month's provisions aboard and sank a Turkish minelayer above the Narrows.

Rabbit Island reported to be full of wounded, and anchored off are four or five hospital ships; two hospital ships proceeding full speed for Malta.

The following signal reached us: 'During the day 33,000 British and 3,000 French troops were landed, and altogether there were 5,000 casualties on our side.'

MONDAY APRIL 26TH. Rifle-fire most of the night. At 1 a.m. the position of our troops on Gallipoli was very critical. French troops still landing horses, stores and guns at Kum Kale.

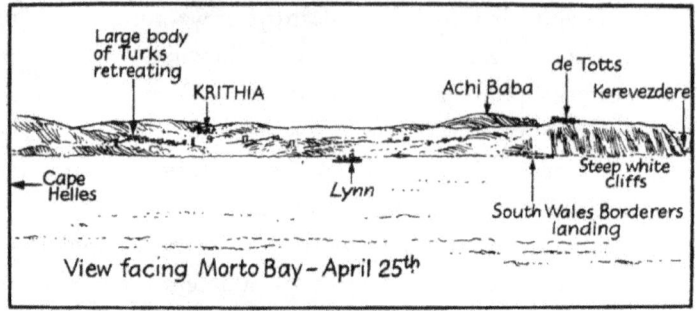

Gallipoli Shore: Morto Bay from author's sketch

At 7.30 a.m. entered the Straits when snipers started potting at us again, so we had to keep under cover. 9.30. Ran up Straits supporting sweeping destroyers, as far as Domuz Deresi; they were fired on by shrapnel from Asian shore. While they had a whack at us — about half a dozen 8-in. howitzers from Suan Dere (some of them within 20 ft of us) — we could see a small tug alongside the stranded *E 15*. About four of our ships inside the Straits shelling enemy's positions both sides.

At 11 a.m. we did another run-up but turned to port this time; thus we rather upset our friend's calculations so that he failed to make good practice on us. At 12.30 on our return run we had a splendid view of our fellows at Seddul Bahr potting away at enemy.

Went up again with destroyers and shelled Turkish ships at Chanak, but when a little further up than our usual turning point destroyers suddenly caught three mines in their sweeps and brought them to the surface about 300 or 400 yds ahead of us; we put our helm hard over and turned round while everyone blazed away at them; they looked pretty new mines, copper, fairly bright and very big. After firing rifles, Maxims and guns at the mines one exploded with a huge splash at 2.12 p.m. Two others were sunk later but did not explode; we must have been very near the minefield where we usually turn and that is probably why they never fired on us until we turned, so as to lure us onto the minefield. Destroyers dropped a mark-buoy at the end of the minefield. French minesweepers, sweeping the Asiatic side, were being fired on from Aren Kioi.

4 p.m. Opened fire with 12-pdrs on Turks retreating across Morto Bay and killed about a dozen or two hiding behind trees by rapid fire. Our troops are now in the old Fort 2 on top of Seddul Bahr. 5 p.m. Howitzers on Kum Kale side firing on French in No. 6 Fort; all ships replying temporarily silencing guns. At 7.40 we proceeded out of Straits to patrol off 'Y' Beach.

To provide necessary support for the troops when required half our armament had to be manned all night while the other half of us slept below. The only trouble for the sleepers was that every time a gun fired, the marauding cockroaches crawling overhead would be shaken off and fall upon us still asleep in our hammocks beneath.

Other events today: *E 14* left with one month's provisions for Sea of Marmara. *Queen Elizabeth* sank Turkish transport in four shots by indirect fire: first shot 300 over, second 50 short, third hit and fourth sank her.

During the night the French troops evacuated Kum Kale with all their guns, stores, etc., and continued to land again at 'V' Beach Seddul Bahr in accordance with plan.

The French landing on the Asian shore had been part of a feint to deceive the Turks. Another feint landing was also made at Bulair.

TUESDAY APRIL 27TH. At 7 a.m. entered the Straits. Went to Action Stations and at 9 a.m. we did a run-up with the sweeping destroyers and got fired on pretty close by 'Archie' (we gave all the enemy howitzer guns nicknames) getting a straddle of five. Destroyers ahead of us caught a couple of mines which exploded in their sweep.

Engaged Asiatic battery with 9.2-in. guns during the forenoon and did another run-up with destroyers, but not so successful as some of the sweeps parted.

At noon I saw some Turkish prisoners at De Totts being made to cart up stores, ammunition, etc. The French troops are advancing across the plateau in Morto Bay without any opposition and soon ought to join our fellows at De Totts.

At 12.30 we did another run-up with destroyers who swept exactly 2 miles further up than where the first mines were discovered, past Domuz Deresi; they were fired on heavily by shrapnel from Suan Dere and had men wounded. *Grampus* caught a mine which exploded in her sweep. Before turning back we fired five rounds with our fore turret at Chanak, range 20,000 yds, but all fell short in the water. We could see a couple of T.B.s up there patrolling and a destroyer well beyond Chanak. On our return run, the Asian howitzers, 'Archie' and his brothers, did very good practice on us being within 10 and 20 yds away, and fired about eight or 10 rounds with the usual 8-in. high-explosive howitzers.

2.30. Opened fire with port 12-pdrs on Turks retreating at back of Morto Bay and over the ridge. At 4 p.m. we did another run-up with the destroyers but *Racoon* and *Mosquito* got hit in the main steam-pipes and had to blow off steam. *Racoon* came alongside later for small repair under our lee. After this we did no more firing or running up, but proceeded to 'Y' Beach. Not much activity all day, a little rifle-fire and things were fairly quiet.

Off Cape Helles there are now about 80 transports lying at anchor; one might be at some big docks: tugs, steam-boats, etc., rushing about as though it were the Thames; certainly a wonderful sight. All French ships now clear of Kum Kale, their evacuation of the Asian shore now being complete.

WEDNESDAY APRIL 28TH. Got turned out at 6 a.m. for 'Action' and proceeded up the Straits with sweeping destroyers, but unfortunately *Wolverine* got struck by a small shell on the bridge, killing Captain, Midshipman R.N.R. and Gunner, two men, and wounding three others. Sweeping was temporarily abandoned, and we returned to entrance while *Wolverine* transferred her killed and wounded to hospital ship. We proceed to *Queen Elizabeth* off Cape Helles to enable Captain Heneage (in charge minesweeping) to see the Admiral. (It could have been to point out the exposed position of the destroyers completely unprotected from shrapnel-fire. We hoped so.) We went very close to *Q.E.* and saw on the quarterdeck Sir Ian Hamilton, the French General d'Amade and many staff officers, but not Commodore Keyes, the active Chief of Staff.

We then proceeded back to the Straits to support troops on our right flank for at 10 a.m. Achi Baba batteries were shelling them and our batteries replying. Musketry active with a big battle going on and our troops trying to advance, and the French on our right flank seemed to be succeeding.

At 1.30 p.m. saw *Nellie* rather far up under fire of 'Archie', and at 2.15 the Russian *Askold* was supporting minesweepers on the Asiatic shore with *Prince George* and *Henri IV*. After firing a few rounds from P 1 and the fore turret at Turks retreating on Halar Road, some small field-guns opened fire on us from Asia forcing us to take cover. This does not affect me as I am in the top nearly all day, but those having their afternoon siesta nearly got shut down. We went up the Straits to entice No. 8 Fort to fire on us but, of course, he refused, and 'Archie' did instead, but he can never be located.

At 6 p.m. off the Gallipoli shore. We opened fire on Turks with 12-pdrs in the next valley past De Totts battery. I could see a dozen of them rush out of their trench, run 50 yds, lie flat with our men's rifle-bullet splashes all round them. When we directed our fire at them I saw a lot of heads, legs and arms go up in the air; however they fought very bravely and made a very good effort to rush the French trenches, and no doubt would have succeeded had it not been for us. Then their snipers in the valley tried to be funny by firing bullets over the quarterdeck and forcing everyone under cover. Then a few shells reached us and later they had the impertinence to turn a Maxim on the quarterdeck.

Cornwallis, *Prince George* and *Lord Nelson* now opened fire on the Turks just where we had, but the French Zouaves (or Senegalese troops), conspicuous in blue uniform, absolutely gave way and retreated in great disorder losing many under a heavy shrapnel fire. I remember seeing one gallant little French officer, who, whilst running in retreat, would stop at intervals and, entirely on his own, fire from the kneeling position at the advancing Turks. 'Why weren't we supporting our Allies with *Agamemnon*'s guns?' was the question on our conscience and voiced loudly by our gunnery officer and Lt Crookshank. Alas, Fluter had let the ship get swept round by the current so that our guns couldn't bear. He took so long to get her back that the opportunity was lost. A very bad show on our part. A lot of the colonials, in the panic, ran down to the boats which had been sent in for wounded. Some men now pretended that they were wounded, but they were detected and shot on the spot; others later for cowardice. A couple of R.N.R. lieutenants from the net-layer *Lynn* in Morto Bay tried to chase them back with sticks and partially succeeded. Later in the evening they took up a retired position in good order.

At 7.15 we steamed out of the Straits and took station for the night off 'Y' Beach. Big fire observed at Maidos, the Turkish headquarters, where our aeroplane had made a raid and dropped several bombs.

Turkish prisoner reports that one of *Queen Elizabeth*'s shrapnel shells killed nearly a whole battalion of Turks.

THURSDAY APRIL 29TH. Did not sound off 'Action' till 10.15 when 'Spiteful William' opened fire on us so we had to get under cover. Another beautiful day and though the summer weather seems pretty settled, today it is blowing fairly hard from the N.E. Pretty quiet ashore on the whole; no firing audible at all and our fellows seem to be digging themselves in all day.

At 12.15 port 9.2 guns and fore turret opened fire on the Krithia windmills where 2,000 Turkish reinforcements were reported to be coming up. At 2.45 *Agamemnon* and *Lord Nelson* went up the Straits to have another look for 'Archie', but meanwhile we were hit starb. side for'd of flying deck, the shell making a large hole and melting anything near it. The shell splinters also made decent-sized holes, thus showing that explosion was really violent though the bits of shell were of minute size; the motor bollard and 12-pdr mountings were slightly damaged: about five other shots straddled us. *Lord Nelson* also got fired on, but owing to superior manoeuvring she was not hit.

At 5 p.m. '*Queen Bess*', with kite-balloon spotting, opened fire on 'Archie', but when we went up to draw fire, 'Artful Archie' would not fire at all, so they came to the foolish conclusion that he was knocked out. At 7 p.m. our howitzers at Seddul

Bahr started bombarding the enemy's trenches with shrapnel and field-guns joined in. Just as we were steaming out of the Straits, we heard the 'Charge' sound ashore, and saw the French chaps all leap out and charge.

Agamemnon then crashed through the anchorage at 10 knots when, suddenly, we went full speed astern and there was a slight bump. When I came up on deck I found everyone dashing about throwing all floatable matter in the water to about 20 soldiers and others who had jumped from a trawler we had rammed, but not sunk. After a while they were all saved by picket-boats, etc., except for one man who was drowned. We then proceeded to 'Y' Beach after getting a rebuking and insulting message from Admiral Wemyss in *Euryalus*.

We left a big fire burning in Krithia.

FRIDAY APRIL 30TH. Entered Straits and at 6.30 found Seddul Bahr being shelled from Asia by field-guns at extreme range; some shells dropping on lighters and stores, though the anchorage has fewer ships. At 9.30 went to Action Stations and, in conjunction with other ships, we silenced the four field-guns, which are very hard to hit as only the tips of the muzzles are shown when they fire. At 10 a.m. P 1 fired on the 'square'[4] as ordered.

Vengeance was in her old position in the bay N.W of De Totts and getting fired on frequently by 'Artful Archie'. *Henri IV* got fired on occasionally by 'Morbid Montmorentzi'. At 10.15 aeroplane up spotting for our fire on howitzer guns.

---

[4] The 'square', so frequently referred to as our target, was a small area on a military map, e.g. 'Fire on square 4g 5Q' would indicate where we should aim to drop our shells.

In the afternoon fore turret fired on 'square' by order. At 5 p.m. sighted hostile aeroplane bearing N. W., but was very high and returned towards Chanak. Balloon ship *Manica* suddenly got fired on by our Asiatic friends and had to haul down balloon and proceed out of it. At 6 p.m. our shore howitzers and *Cornwallis* opened fire on Asiatic battery.

This afternoon *Lord Nelson*, off Gaba Tepe with balloon spotting, opened indirect fire at *Goeben* at Chanak, but the latter made off at full speed after five rounds. *Nellie* then fired on German H.Q. at Chanak and made a bonfire which burnt all night long. Just before leaving at 7 p.m. I saw a spy-hunt in Morto Bay and could see the spy fairly running away, sacrificing his clothes to gain speed.

At 7 p.m. we proceeded to Tenedos and I had to go away in the whaler to take the Sperry compass man to *Adamant* (depot ship) and also to get stores: however I got back by 11.30 p.m. (We had constant trouble with one new gyro compass.)

Some interesting enemy dispatches have been found at Seddul Bahr, referring to General Liman von Saunders, Comm. in Chief 3rd Army. The Turks evidently put great faith in him and he wrote one very patriotic memo, thoroughly convincing them that the British could not possibly land. They only believed we might attempt to land at 'W', 'V', and Morto Bay (not De Totts, where we actually did), at Domuz Deresi and also at Gaba Tepe.

SATURDAY MAY 1ST. Proceeded up Straits as usual and at 9 a.m. we had to sound off Action as 'Whistling Rufus' started throwing a few pebbles at us. Also a few 'big stuff' went right over us and pitched very close to the net-steamer *Lynn* in Morto Bay.

At 11 a.m. the air-chamber of a torpedo was sighted floating down with the tide and was identified as belonging to the French submarine *Joule*, which left early for a reconnaissance this morning, so we concluded she must have foundered; our conclusion was soon confirmed for we heard she ran on a mine at the Narrows.

I have now got a new job: to look out for mines from the crow's-nest. Every time a gun fires the mast wobbles so much that I am nearly thrown into the ditch.

At 5 p.m. we loosed off a few more rounds of 9.2-in. at Asiatic batteries, but at 6 p.m. 'Whistling Rufus', 'Morbid Montmorentzi',[5] etc., were all going strong so we fired some more 9.2, shrapnel as well this time, and shut them up. 6.30 p.m. Hostile aeroplane up at great height but later made off again for Chanak. We soon proceeded out of Straits to our usual billet off 'Y' for the night.

During the 1st Watch there was a fierce battle going on with star shells, rockets and the very devil of a noise — really a fine sight for me, but probably not so for the soldiers. Commander Sampson flew over Chanak in the afternoon, dropping some bombs which caused a big fire burning all night.

Early part of the night the French retreated right back into Morto Bay with great loss and a little later the Naval Brigade came up and recaptured all the lost trenches.

Australian submarine *AE 2* reported off Constantinople.

SUNDAY MAY 2ND. After a hard-worked Middle Watch, turned out at 5.30 to go to Action Stations in order to support our right flank. Fierce battle going on most of the night. We opened fire on Turks with P 1 turret and 12-pdrs to help one

---

[5] Our names for the concealed enemy mobile guns on the Asian shore were liable to slight changes.

of our batteries during the Middle Watch.

At 6 a.m. Frenchmen were retreating on top of cliffs under a murderous fire of shrapnel from Turkish field-battery, now under our observation. We accordingly opened fire with 12-pdrs and P 2; one good salvo eventually silenced the battery. All of a sudden 'Archie' opened fire on our old mark buoy off Domuz Deresi and fired about 40 rounds evidently mistaking it for a submarine. *Albion* and *Vengeance* with us and being fired on by 'Archie'. Shrapnel bursting very close to us, the bursts spluttering in the water all round us. However we managed to get down for some breakfast at 8 a.m. At 8.30 the after turret opened fire on battery at Kum Kale with the aeroplane spotting and getting a rotten time from their anti-aircraft guns. After 26 rounds the aeroplane reported three guns knocked out; then we fired 16 more rounds at another gun. *Prince George* was bombarding Asiatic shore all the forenoon.

At noon we were ordered to bombard Krithia, but we took such a long time getting into station that *Goliath* did it for us. 1 p.m. *Albion* was getting fired on by 'Archie' and hit twice.

In the afternoon Dr Spalding landed with Sick Berth staff to attend to French wounded at the foot of De Totts battery and he came back later with much loot and rifles. At 6 p.m. 'Morose Montmorentzi' opened fire on De Totts so we shut him up by firing S 2 turret. At 7 p.m. fierce musketry going on and shrapnel bursting over trawlers with wounded. Proceeded out of Straits as usual. Six of our cutter's crew are missing; three are killed.

Reported Australian submarine *AE* 2 had been rammed and sunk by a Turkish T.B., many being saved.

MONDAY MAY 3RD. Entered Straits to find our howitzer friends potting away at *Prince George* and they succeeded in hitting her twice, once on the anchor-bed and once on the waterline. At 8.45 went to Action Stations. *Goliath* got hit between the funnels by 'Archie'. We opened fire with the after turret on Asiatic battery, but, having fired 48 rounds our aeroplane informed us we had knocked out one gun out of a battery of four. *Prince George* left for Mudros for repairs to her hole in the waterline.

At 2 p.m. sweeping destroyers met outside and we proceeded up the Straits with four pairs of sweeps to make sure of the original swept area. At 4 p.m. we did another run-up to widen the swept area; field-guns did not fire shrapnel this time as we expected, probably because we took the precaution of clearing the tops!

At 5.30 the *Lord Nelson*, having coaled and ammunitioned, came and relieved us after our 10 days up the Straits. Everyone is looking forward to a rest, but will we get it? We proceeded to Rabbit Island where collier *Pennmorvak* came alongside.

TUESDAY MAY 4TH. After a Middle Watch turned out at 5.30 to coal ship and worked hard till noon, taking in 850 tons. We then immediately weighed and proceeded to Cape Kephalo where immediately ammunition ship *Tees* came alongside and *Carrigan Head* to fill us up with stores, etc. We continued ammunitioning ship throughout the night till 3.30 a.m. from *Riversdale* and *Swansea Vale* in turn.

That is the end of our 'Rest' and I think it certainly deserves mention to show how hard the ship's company are worked.

WEDNESDAY MAY 5TH. Off 'Y' Beach early and to our great joy found we would not have to go inside the Straits today, but would have to exercise sweepers, destroyer-sweepers and fleet sweepers in tactics and new signal codes. We cruised about off Imbros all day and the hands were actually given a 'Make and Mend'.

We got orders that we would have to look after the Asiatic batteries in future starting tomorrow and going on all day.

Only 13 of our beach party have returned out of 39 that left the ship. *Cornwallis* has lost 50 or 60 of her ship's company which were landed to support the troops; amongst her officers I much regret the loss of poor old Hardiman, who was shot in the stomach and killed instantly: he is the third good fellow in the Hawke term whose death has been much regretted.

Here is a cutting from the *Daily Mail*:

It was a very touch-and-go struggle.
The enemy's machine-guns were too scientifically posted. A long line of men was mown down as by a scythe, but the remainder were not to be denied. Had it not been for those inventions of the Devil — machine guns and barbed wire — we should not have stopped short of the crest of Achi Baba...
The Royal Navy has been father and mother to the Army.
The losses (up to May 5) were very severe:
Officers:
Killed — 177
Wounded — 412
Missing — 13

Other ranks:
Killed — 1,990
Wounded — 7,807
Missing — 3,580

Total:
Killed — 2,167
Wounded — 8,219

Missing — 3,593

Aggregate: 13,970

THURSDAY MAY 6TH. Wind blowing hard from the northwest. Battery at Kum Kale was dropping shells into Seddul Bahr. *Cornwallis* in usual billet off Seddul Bahr anchorage replying. Many of the original transports have left for reinforcements and other ships have arrived in their billets, including *La France* and another big four-funneler.

At 8.30 a.m. sounded off Action. Sweeping destroyers proceeded up ahead of us but our pair fouled their sweep and hoisted two black balls, so sweeping was abandoned and we anchored in Morto Bay. 10.15. Opened fire with the after turret on Asiatic battery and Commander Sampson spotting with great difficulty; 18 rounds were fired and he reported four hits.

At 10.45 our field-guns and howitzers opened fire on enemy trenches. Large reinforcements brought up on our right. Noon. General musketry engagement all along the line with Maxim fire and shrapnel continuously; our fellows advancing all along the line. Ships in Straits supporting *Majestic*, *Jauréguiberry* and *Henry IV* looking after our right flank. At 2 p.m. Banks in 1st picket-boat returned to the ship after 10 days at 'V' Beach landing.

5 p.m. Weighed and drifted down stream but had to loose off some 9.2-in. as our Asiatic friends began to be objectionable again. Our troops during the evening advanced all along, while we proceeded to 'Y' Beach for the night.

FRIDAY MAY 7TH. 8 a.m. Entered Straits to find artillery duel going on with occasional musketry. Went to Action

Stations at 8.30 and then came to anchor in Morto Bay. At 8.45 'Marmaduke' started shelling Seddul Bahr, so the after turret opened fire and later an aeroplane from Tenedos ascended and spotted for us while the after turret fired 40 rounds ¾ charge.

From the crow's-nest I got a good view of the movements of troops and could see Krithia being shelled heavily. *Majestic* was right flank supporting ship and was relieved by *Canopus* at midday.

At 2 p.m. our starboard 12-pdrs tried to drop shells on 'Whistling Rufus'; the aeroplane could not get corrections through so Fluter wasted 100 rounds by his own spotting, e.g. 'Up a shade', 'Down half 25', although we were firing over 7,000 (extreme range) when accuracy is not within 100 yds. At 2.40 shrapnel burst very near our foretop sending bullets ricocheting off the roof, and some in the top, making everyone duck. At 3 p.m. *Canopus* started firing rapidly at running Turks. 'Artful Archie' fired on her, but only one shot at a time and consequently very wide. After tea another aeroplane went up so our after turret opened fire again and wasted a few more rounds, bringing up the total for the day to 63 rounds ¾ charge. During the afternoon there was a fierce artillery duel going on and later our centre advanced and is within 400 yds of Krithia.

This general advance which started yesterday is to capture Achi Baba, but all the way up to the peak is thickly entrenched, otherwise it would have been captured the first two days as was intended. Krithia was expected to fall last night, but our troops cannot enter the village on account of the enemy's well-concealed machine-guns.

At 7 p.m. weighed and proceeded to 'Y' Beach as usual.

SATURDAY MAY 8TH. 8.30 a.m. Entered Straits and

sounded off 'Action'. Came to anchor in Morto Bay at 8.45: beautiful warm weather again and things pretty quiet. At 9 a.m. aeroplane ascended from Seddul Bahr to spot for us, and we opened fire with 12-pdrs on three concealed field-guns all of the 'Whistling Rufus' type. We ceased firing after having fired 180 rounds. 11.30. Sighted enemy aeroplane over Seddul Bahr trying to drop bombs on kite-balloon, but it was driven off by our shrapnel at 11.45 and one of our machines chased after him. We again opened fire and continued till 1.30 with aeroplane spotting and got through 440 rounds. 2 p.m. Big Asiatic 'Jack Johnson'[6] fired on De Totts battery, so we silenced him with five rounds from S 2. 'Archie' opened fire on *Henri IV* but did not hit.

In the afternoon we opened fire with S 2, aeroplane spotting, and fired 33 rounds till 4.20 p.m. At 4 p.m. sighted float of Electro-Contact mine drifting down stream; *Savage* went to engage mine and sank it.

At 5.30 rapid artillery and rifle fire: furious assaults and our people trying to advance on centre and right. Frenchmen advancing in mass but can see hundreds falling by enemy shrapnel. We fired a few more rounds with S 2 at Asia and then went to 'Y' Beach for the night.

SUNDAY MAY 9TH. 5.30. Came to anchor off Cape Helles in order to change places with *Implacable*. We have two turret-crews completely closed up and ready to open fire; also we send Mr Holmes and Gardner as beach officers. Very peaceful day, Sunday routine and church — the first 'Sunday' for months.

Wounded being brought off to hospital ships had to be returned to the shore as there was no more room. Some of

---

[6] Big, black, bursting H.E. shells, named after the famous boxer.

them had hardly been attended to for 20 hours and had had no food.

E 14 reports expending all her torpedoes and is on the home voyage, having torpedoed two gunboats and one transport.

Reported that the *Lusitania* has been torpedoed off Kinsale with 1,900 passengers and crew of which 1,200 were lost.

W/T signal from Constantinople to BQ (*Agamemnon*): 'Schweinhund!' (N.B. This may be the enemy trying to be funny to us or else a code-word to *Goeben*.)

MONDAY MAY 10TH. Off Cape Helles: another peaceful day at anchor. In the afternoon I had a look at 'W' and 'X' Beaches in the picket-boat as Fluter landed to collect loot.

All ammunition and supply ships are ordered to be in Port Mudros by tomorrow night on account of the approach of hostile submarines which are soon due. Nets to protect merchantmen are being provided at Cape Kephalo, Mudros and at Tenedos.

3.30 p.m. *Baron Ardrossan* came alongside and we took in 89 common 9.2-in., five shrapnel and 28 Trotyl (a new high-explosive). At 6p.m. we weighed and proceeded to Cape Kephalo anchorage, Imbros, where *Tees* came alongside and we took in more ammunition.

TUESDAY MAY 11TH. Weighed at 5.30 a.m. and proceeded Cape Helles to coal. At 9.10 *Barrington Court* came alongside and we took in 420 tons of coal with three, sometimes two holds working. Asiatic batteries dropping many shells into Seddul Bahr, and *Implacable*, being new on the job, cannot stop them, so the Admiral has ordered us to resume our original jobs this morning.

Special patrols have been organised to intercept the hostile submarines from getting to Smyrna or here. Searchlight signals made *en claire* in the vicinity of the Straits are in future prohibited.

Reported that three of our secret codes have been compromised.

WEDNESDAY MAY 12TH. Weighed at 8 a.m. and proceeded up the Straits to usual anchorage in Morto Bay. Weather very poor for firing.

Many transports have left here to fetch more troops, some for the safety of Mudros on account of submarine danger. An aeroplane is to be up all day and the Admiral will hoist his flag in *Dublin* when a submarine is sighted. *Queen Elizabeth* will leave for Port Mudros and it is expected she will go home.

No activity at all during the day till later on. At 2 p.m. weather cleared so *Cornwallis* opened fire on the town of Halar. 'Archie' retaliated by firing on the old *Jauréguiberry*. At 6.30 our field-guns started artillery attack, followed up as usual by rifle firing. We weighed and proceeded to 'X' Beach.

THURSDAY MAY 13TH. At about 1.15 a.m. it was realised that the battleship *Goliath*, anchored in our usual berth in Morto Bay, was in trouble. *Cornwallis*, anchored some distance astern, had heard three dull thuds and, after hearing yells from men struggling in the water as they were swept past her by the current, realised that *Goliath* had been torpedoed and sunk.[7]

All ships were informed, weighed anchor and proceeded seawards.

---

[7] The wreck of *Goliath* now lies in position 40° 02' 22"N, 26° 12' 23"E, very broken up and largely salvaged.

Although Cornwallis *soon got out her boats to rescue survivors, less than 200 were saved of a complement of about 800. Later we learnt that the ship was sunk by the Turkish torpedo-boat* Muavanet *(with a German officer's help) which had eluded our patrol destroyers by creeping down the Gallipoli shore towards the entrance of Morto Bay.*

At 9.30 a.m. we anchored off Kum Kale village and opened fire on an Asiatic battery with a 'nine-two', but, after a couple of rounds, we shifted to a new target — a howitzer which had begun to shell Seddul Bahr beach. With aeroplane spotting we fired 35 rounds of 9.2-in. We hoisted out our picket-boat in a strong tideway to spot for floating mines.

11.40. Weighed and proceeded to station off Seddul Bahr and again anchored with nets out. During the afternoon several shells were dropped on 'W' Beach and roundabout, killing 40 horses and some men. At 5 p.m. a small field gun from Asia tried to drop shells on *River Clyde*, but it seemed to be extreme range and no hits were obtained. *Cornwallis*, *Vengeance* and *Jauréguiberry* replied, also one of the French howitzers. 5.15 p.m. We opened fire on it with starboard 'nine-twos'; 42 rounds were fired and the shooting was good. *Swiftsure* tried to drop big shells into 'Archie' at Suan Dere but she fired about 14 rounds in the sea over the point. At 7.15 p.m. we weighed and proceeded to 'X' Beach and came to anchor with our nets out.

Later, the Gurkhas made a small advance of 300 yds and captured an important ravine on our left flank.

FRIDAY MAY 14TH. In the Dardanelles: at 9.30 a.m. came to anchor one mile off Kum Kale with our nets out again. At 10 a.m. aeroplane reported it being very hazy, but at 10.15 S 3 opened fire on square 155 L3 with ½ charges. Rippling salvoes (eight) of shrapnel being fired over Seddul Bahr (from 177 W). These were subsequently silenced by French field-guns. At

11.40 we ceased firing, having fired 33 rounds, and aeroplane reported five direct hits. We then weighed and proceeded to anchorage off 'Y' Beach; fore turret opened fire on 'Archie' (178 K) full charge 12,500 yds with aeroplane up spotting. At 3.45 we ceased firing, having fired 40 rounds, weighed and proceeded to this morning's billet off Kum Kale and came to anchor at 5.20.

Urgent W/T signal from Tenedos to Admiral: '5 submarines reported 3 miles below Kephez Point.' This caused a certain amount of excitement at the time but later it was discovered to be the wash of the Turkish mark buoys. Shrapnel still being fired over Seddul Bahr, big 'Black Johnsons'. 6.30. Asiastic battery fired at *Vengeance* and hit her once; we fired S 3 and silenced battery aided by *Vengeance*. At 7 p.m. we weighed and proceeded to 'X' Beach where we anchored for the night with nets out as usual.

SATURDAY MAY 15TH. Weighed and proceeded further along the coast off 'Y' Beach and anchored again at 9.30 in order to fire on square (178 K4). At 10.15 the fore turret opened fire with aeroplane spotting; the aeroplane was getting more shrapnel than he wanted. Aeroplane used coloured smokes for signals as a precaution when the wireless fails. Fired 14 full charge, got one O.K. and eight within 30 yds; aeroplane returned at 11.20.

At 2.15 aeroplane was again in position and the after turret opened fire full charge firing 27 altogether till 3.30, when we furled nets and weighed. Aeroplane then asked us to fire on square (184 Z) Krithia road which we did with 12-pdrs and fired rapidly; aeroplane reported we damaged camp and stampeded horses.

5.20. We came to anchor 1 mile south of Seddul Bahr to find *Cornwallis* having a warm time in Morto Bay. 5.30. Message from Conning Tower to Foretop: 'Aeroplane over us dropping bombs.' It was really funny to see people gingerly putting their heads out of the top. Anyhow he dropped two bombs, one in the ditch and one not far from our aeroplanes at Seddul Bahr, which should make a big enough target for him. He then made off with a couple of our machines in chase of him, but he was very high up and our machines could only watch where he landed. We then opened fire with S 2 turret on Asiatic battery square (155 L3). 5.40. *Canopus* closed Asiatic shore and fired on battery in 15U V9, near 'Whistling Rufus'. At 6.15 we checked fire as aeroplane returned. 6.45. *Canopus* firing rapidly with 6-in. guns into valley, probably at retreating Turks. 'Archie' fired at her three or four times.

At 7 p.m. we ceased firing after 25 rounds from S 3, and proceeded to our usual night anchorage off 'X' Beach with nets out.

SUNDAY MAY 16TH. Off the Entrance: anchored at 9a.m. off Kum Kale and found gun (in 159 X) firing at *Majestic*. An attempt by the Turks to draw fire at the wrong place was made by means of a dummy gun which made a big cloud of smoke, concealing the flash of the proper gun. It was a poor attempt and did not deceive us in any way.

9.30. *Albion* and *Majestic* were getting fired on again and latter got hit; 'Archie' also fired at her. At 10.15 our aeroplane being up we opened fire on 160 V2 till 11.30 when aeroplane returned after S 1 had fired 23 rounds full charge. Seddul Bahr being shelled again during forenoon by big black shrapnel. 2 p.m. Aeroplane up again and so S 1 opened fire again, same object. Anti-aircraft guns firing salvoes of 4 at our machine, so

Canopus engaged them and silenced them. 3.30. Ceased firing after 38 rounds.

At 5.15 Lt Murray went in picket-boat up to Domuz Deresi to look at anti-mine net, and got fired on a few times from Aren Kioi by field-guns.

At 5.30 we opened fire with S 3 ½-charges on square 155 L3 but aeroplane put us on the dummy guns. 6.30. Ceased firing and at 7 p.m. we weighed and proceeded to our usual anchorage off 'X' Beach for the night.

MONDAY MAY 17TH. 6.45 a.m. Came to anchor off Seddul Bahr in position for right flank supporting ship. 10.30. Asiatic battery fired a few rounds of small stuff at us, but was soon silenced by a couple of rounds from S 3 assisted by *Albion*. Shrapnel fired at 'W' Beach (from position 177 W) was silenced by *Albion* and French field-guns. Very quiet day on the whole.

7 p.m. We weighed and proceeded to usual night anchorage.

At 3 a.m. this morning two trawlers reported sighting hostile submarine off Rabbit Island.

Personal note: It is rumoured that the Parson has been trying to rebuke old Fluter about the insolent and ill-mannered way he treats his officers. According to the Chief Yeoman this is the effect: "E 'ad 'ardly any breakfast; 'e says thankee to 'is stooard, 'aw 'e gives 'is coxswain 'alf a day orf, a thing 'e never done before.'

TUESDAY MAY 18TH. Off Seddul Bahr, supporting ship: at 6.30 we came to anchor off 'V' Beach. Nothing at all happened during the forenoon. At 1.30 the French *Saint Louis* ran up as far as Domuz Deresi and, of course, 'Archie' had half a dozen shots at her, but by very good manoeuvring no hits were obtained. At 2.45 our French Seddul Bahr howitzers opened fire on Turkish long-range artillery. 3 p.m. Big howitzer shells being dropped on Seddul Bahr village and on 'V' Beach.

At 3.15 Yeoman Grant, who was keeping a very sharp lookout for floating objects, sighted a floating contact mine drifting down, which was very difficult to distinguish owing to its colour and to the rough state of the sea. However we got guns ready for sinking mine and sent picket-boat away with net.

At 3.25 when no one was looking, submarine *E 14* (Lt-Comdr Boyle) suddenly broke surface between us and the *Saint Louis*, very close to the latter who cheered her loudly. She then proceeded to Cape Kephalo flying the skull and cross-bones; she has been up the Dardanelles for three weeks and one day. During her time up there besides what she 'fished' she passed many empty transports which she let go, also refugee ships which she made heave to and then let carry on; the latter always cheered her loudly. *E 14* on her downward journey stopped off Chanak, and under heavy fire and bothered by sweeps all the time; she counted 60 guns there.

At 3.28 we opened fire on mine with P 1 12-pdr; picket-boat engaged it with 3-pdr at close range. 3.38. Eventually mine sank by concussion of so many shots bursting close to it from P 1; also many shots ricocheted and landed very close to 'U' Beach.

After tea we opened fire by order with fore turret and P 1 on Achi Baba: unfortunately, one shot from P 1 landed right into the French troops above De Totts but luckily did not kill any. (Sight-setter had put on 3,800 yds instead of 10,800.)

During the Dog Watches we played deck hockey while under fire from 'Whistling Rufus', but he soon shut up after three or four rounds.

At 7 p.m. we weighed and proceeded to anchorage 'W' Beach for the night.

WEDNESDAY MAY 19TH. 'W' Beach to Mudros. At 1.15 a.m. submarine *E 11* proceeded up the Straits with 14 torpedoes.

We are to have a stand-off today or, at any rate, during the forenoon. At 2.15 p.m. we weighed and proceeded to Mudros where we got a big mail of 36 bags. Collier and storeship came alongside later.

THURSDAY MAY 20TH. Turned out at 6.30 to start coaling from collier *Darnholme*: at 10.15 we ceased having taken in 650 tons. In the afternoon we took in a lot of ammunition from *Swansea Vale*, also some of various sorts from *Swanley*, which the gunnery officer complains is very badly stowed.

All the officers went for picnics. I went with Fluter's picnic and really we had quite a good time. We finished up with a two-mile swim and then a big tea with plenty of sloe gin.

Tonight the Turks are reported to have made a vigorous attack on the Australians at Gaba Tepe, but the former have apparently lost 7,000 of which we have seen 2,000 dead and our people lost 800 only.

FRIDAY MAY 21ST. At noon the ship weighed and we proceeded to Cape Tekeh at 14 knots, owing to submarines being reported in the vicinity of north Aegean. Came to anchor at 4 p.m. and got out our nets.

S. Taylor returned in 2nd picket-boat which was in a sinking condition and had to be hoisted in. Anyhow, he relieves me at Action Stations in the top and I now go back to the after turret.

SATURDAY MAY 22ND. Right flank supporting ship. Weighed at 5.30 a.m. to take station off Seddul Bahr where we came to anchor with our nets out. During the day we fired a few rounds with the fore turret on a 'square' in line with Achi Baba, also a few rounds at Asiatic batteries which fired at us. *Prince George* and *Cornwallis* both got hit by the Asiatic battery, the former ship having one killed and a few wounded.

In the afternoon *Prince George* reported hostile submarine off Gaba Tepe, so all ships — merchantmen and everyone — weighed, except *Agamemnon* who had nets out. Report was eventually considered doubtful, but the anchorage off Cape Helles was now empty for the first time since landing; only a couple of small coasters left.

Albion ran aground at Gaba Tepe and *Lord Nelson* and *Canopus* are looking after her. 7 p.m. Weighed and proceeded off 'W' Beach as usual.

SUNDAY MAY 23RD. Right flank supporting ship. Weighed at 6 a.m. and proceeded to entrance off Seddul Bahr. 8.45. Sounded off Action and we went further up Straits. Asiatic battery fired a few rounds at us but was soon silenced by S 3. We then fired a few rounds with the fore turret on 'square' near Achi Baba.

At 9.15 a.m. *Canopus* towed *Albion* off at Gaba Tepe after the former had been hit a good many times and had had one man killed and 10 wounded. She left later for Malta.

At 1 p.m. *Prince George* came up the Straits and relieved us, so we proceeded to anchorage off Cape Helles with our nets out. End of day's work.

In the Dog Watches we had a decent bathe. In the afternoon we had an aeroplane scare and mistook one of our machines, which was very high, for the enemy and nearly fired on it.

MONDAY MAY 24TH. 6.a.m. Entered the Straits and took up our position, but nothing at all happened during the whole forenoon, except that we fired a few 12-in. shell on a 'square'. 'Whistling Rufus' had one shot at us but was unsuccessful in drawing our fire. At 1 p.m. *Majestic* relieved us, so we went to our anchorage off Cape Helles with nets out. 4 p.m. Signal that Italy has declared war on Austria.

The Australians had an armistice from 7.30 a.m. to 5.30 p.m. to bury the dead after the fierce attack on the 20th. Reported *E 11* has sunk large transport in Sea of Marmara.

TUESDAY MAY 25TH. Off Seddul Bahr: at 7.21 a.m. the periscope of a hostile submarine was sighted by one of our destroyers, less than a mile from us, and at 7.30, a little nearer to us, by a trawler. This news was greeted with cheers, loud and prolonged, by everyone in the bathroom. Suddenly at 7.45 the submarine showed her periscope 400 yds off our port quarter between us and *Swiftsure*, three or four times evidently getting in position to loose off, but luckily *Swiftsure* fired a couple of rounds so close that he had to clear out of it and was later observed to be proceeding N. W. up the coast to Gaba Tepe. Conditions for submarine very bad, flat calm, no wind and clear water. Later, we weighed and proceeded up the Straits and at 10.15 opened fire on Asiatic battery, with aeroplane spotting. 12.45 p.m. Signal from RA3[8] to *Agamemnon*: '*Triumph* sunk at 12.30 by enemy submarine.'

---

[8] Rear-Admiral, 3rd Division.

It appears she was struck by two torpedoes, both going through her nets; she capsized after quarter of an hour and sank in half an hour, losing about 50 men, including Eng. Commander. She was also surrounded by destroyers, and an aeroplane was up looking for the submarine. A torpedo had previously been fired at *Vengeance*, but fortunately missed.

At 3 p.m. we were ordered to weigh and proceed to Mudros, so at 3.45 we got in net defence and proceeded at 16 knots zigzagging via Tenedos and to the east of Rabbit Island. At 2.30 aeroplane reported submarine proceeding down coast again, also *Talbot* and *Vengeance* reported her. *Vengeance* avoided being hit by good manoeuvring. 7.30. Arrived Mudros and got out nets.

Author's sketch of first sighting of an enemy periscope, prior to the submarine sinking HMS *Triumph*

NINE: *AGAMEMNON* REFITS AT MALTA

WEDNESDAY MAY 26TH. 6.30 a.m. Started coaling from *Darnholme*, taking in 350 tons. Ammunitioned from *Swansea Vale* and took aboard a new 12-pdr gun.

2.30 p.m. Ordered to proceed to Malta, much to everyone's joy. At 4.30 we weighed and proceeded out of Mudros at 14 knots. *Venerable* arrived and we passed *Exmouth* at 5.30 coming in. We passed through the Doro Channel at midnight and thence through the Zea Channel. Beautiful, calm sea and fine night with a fair moon.

We are giving *Inflexible*'s marines a passage to Malta; from there they are going to join their ship at Gib. They have been manning the guns at the entrance of Port Mudros.

THURSDAY MAY 27TH. From Mudros to Malta: another beautiful day at sea. Passed out of the Aegean through the Kithera Channel and were off C. Matapan at noon. We zigzagged one point either side, altering course every four hours, but most of us felt it should have been far more frequent. At 1.15 steadied on N 84 N direct course for Malta. Hands got a 'Make and Mend' for a change.

FRIDAY MAY 28TH. Arriving at Malta. Another nice day and still steady on N 84 W. We saw nothing all day till we sighted Malta at 2 p.m. when we started to zigzag and were escorted by some French T.B.s as far as the harbour which we entered at 10 knots. During the afternoon we had all 'deadlights' down and men standing by to close W/T doors in case of submarine attack. Just before entering the harbour we zigzagged 4 points either side every 5 and 10 minutes alternately. At 4 p.m. we entered Grand Harbour and at 4.30 we secured alongside Somerset Wharf, and immediately dockyard hands started on the repairs. The new hydraulic engine was hoisted aboard in parts. Leave granted to one watch from 7 p.m. to 7 a.m. tomorrow.

Heard the news of *Majestic* being torpedoed early yesterday morning off Cape Helles, saving all officers and nearly all the men. She was probably still anchored where we left her with nets out; she apparently sank very quickly, capsizing in under 5 minutes, and those who were lost got entangled under her nets as she rolled over and sank.

In port we found the following ships:
British: Albion, *in dry dock having waterline shell-holes repaired;* Harrier, *gunboat on patrol duty;* Renard *and* Mosquito *(destroyers) in dry dock; submarines* B 11, E 7 *and* E 12 *in dry dock.*
French: Courbet, Jean Bart; Paris; France; Danton, Mirabeau, Diderot, Voltaire, Democratie; Verité, République, Patrie; *six destroyers and T.B.s and three submersibles.*

The French ships are looked after by the British dockyards as theirs are so inefficient and their ships get in a very bad state never getting a proper refit. French ships have been withdrawn from the Adriatic owing to the ill feeling between them and Italy.

The next few days I shall cut short as nothing much happened of any interest. I kept out of all social functions and spent most of my time at Tigne bathing when not on watch and before breakfast every day.
  List of British ships that have taken part in the Dardanelles operations during the last four months:

BRITISH SHIPS

BATTLESHIPS
Queen Elizabeth *(gone home)*
Inflexible *(nearly sunk and at Gib.)*
Agamemnon *(damaged; at Malta)*
Lord Nelson
Canopus Cornwallis
Albion *(Malta)*
Vengeance
Prince George
Swiftsure
Venerable *(just come out)*
Exmouth *(just come out)*
Ocean *(sunk)*
Irresistible *(sunk)*
Triumph *(sunk)*
Majestic *(sunk)*
Goliath *(sunk)*
Queen *(Adriatic)*
Prince of Wales *(Adriatic)*
Implacable *(Adriatic)*
London *(Adriatic)*

CRUISERS
Dublin *(Adriatic)*
Amethyst *(Adriatic)*
Sapphire *(Adriatic)*
Minerva
Dartmouth
Talbot
Doris
Cornwall

Europa
Euryalus
Bacchante

Blenheim *(destroyer depot ship)*
Hindo Kuch *(submarine depot ship)*
Ceylon *(submarine depot ship)*
Adamant *(submarine depot ship)*
Ark Royal *(aeroplane carrier: eight machines)*
Reliance *(repair ship)*
Hussar *(gunboat; guardship)*
Triad *(messenger steamer and flagship)*

22 destroyers: 'River'-*class and* 'Beagle'-*class*
Submarines: B 6, B 7, B 8, B 9, B 10 *and* B 11, E 7, E 11, E 12, E 14 *and* E 15 *(sunk);* AE 2 *(sunk)*
Hospital ships: Soudan, Somali, Gascon *and about six or eight army ones*
Ammunition and store ships: Swanley; Carrigan Head; Swansea Vale; Tees, *etc.;* Baron Ardrossan
Fleet Auxiliaries: Colliers: about 25-30, Oilers
Sweepers: Fleet sweepers (eight); eight sweeping destroyers trawlers about 40-50
Aux. vessels: salvage vessels; Linnet and Reclaimer *tugs; water tankers*
About 250 liners have been employed in connection with troops.

FRENCH SHIPS

BATTLESHIPS
Suffren
Charlemagne
Gaulois *(nearly sunk)*
Bouvet *(sunk)*

Henri IV
Jules Fierry *(or one of her class)*
Saint Louis
Massina *(sunk)*

CRUISERS
Julien de Gravière
Jeanne d'Arc
Kléber

SUBMARINES
Coulomb
Joule (sunk)
Bernouille
Circe *and two others*

Four destroyers
Aeroplane ship: Foudre
Sweepers: three (more going)
Auxiliaries: colliers (half a dozen)
Hospital ships: Canada *(four military ones)*
About 40 or 50 of their liners have been used in connection with their troop transport

SATURDAY MAY 29TH. For the next three weeks the ship was thoroughly overhauled, shell-damage repaired, new guns, new funnel, etc. We midshipmen were given a course of instruction but managed to get ashore for swimming, bat fives, driving flat carts, and dining ashore. Altogether have spent £6 and owe £1.

Bad news from the Dardanelles — much German submarine activity.

SATURDAY JUNE 12TH. Our *E 11* arrived for refit after recent operations in Sea of Marmara, having accounted for 10 steamers. She was able to recover some of her torpedoes, which missed the target, by setting them to float rather than the usual practice of their being set to sink. She was nearly blown up on her return voyage by catching a mine wire in her foremast hydroplane; but eventually extricating herself she surfaced near the Entrance on June 7th to be met by *Grampus*.

MONDAY JUNE 21ST. Refit completed. At 6 a.m. dockyard tugs shifted us across the other side to boathouse wharf to make room for the *France* to come under our crane. Heard we were sailing at 5 p.m. so got ashore after lunch for a last decent bathe at Tigne. Took aboard Colonel Sykes, a surgeon, and journalist Ashmead-Barlett.

At 5 p.m. we slipped and three tugs towed us out of the creek into the main channel where we steamed out under our own power, after saluting the Frenchmen and giving them a touch of 'La Marseillaise'. The *Colne* came out to escort us; *Mosquito* with Capt. D (destroyer flotilla) is following later, so a French T.B. came out to escort us for a couple of hours instead. We zigzagged for one hour sometimes 4 points, sometimes less, and then steadied on S 77 E speed 15 knots. Beautiful night; slung hammock on deck.

TUESDAY JUNE 22ND. Returning to Mudros. *Mosquito* joined up during the night. At 1 p.m. we altered course to make the Antikithera Channel; at 11 p.m. we passed through that channel (into the Aegean), land being plainly visible on either side by the bright moon. 11 p.m. a/c to N 28 E which takes us through Thermia Channel and then Doro Channel. We were challenged by the French patrol in Antikithera

Channel.

Colne's wireless broke down so she kept in sight of us, while *Mosquito* went on ahead to examine Thermia Channel. Passed *Swiftsure* during night proceeding to Malta.

WEDNESDAY JUNE 23RD. Beautiful day and no wind. At 9.10 a.m. we passed through Doro Channel which was rather beautiful; it has always been night when we passed through before. Our destroyers examined the coast and looked at all the craft they passed. 3 p.m. Strati Island abeam distant 20 miles, keeping well clear of all land. At 4 p.m. we altered course to N 16 W which brings us right into Mudros.

We got an urgent W/T signal stating that a German submarine was sighted off north Imbros steering east. We started to zigzag and sent destroyers on ahead; we arrived safely at Mudros coming to anchor there at 6.40 p.m. and discharged 400 mail-bags for the fleet to *Europa* for distribution.

There are now many more ships out here than when we left. French ships *Kléber*, *Dupleix*, *Gaulois* (returned after repair), also about 20 French armed drifters and 10 British ones. We have four new armed boarding steamers: *Sardinia*, *Carron*, *Partridge* and *Rowan*, also *Prince of Wales* and *Queen Victoria* (two big paddle net-layers).

THURSDAY JUNE 24TH. Coaled ship, starting early, taking in 650 tons till 2.30 p.m. from collier *England* and at 4 p.m. I went ashore in the cutter and we all bathed.

The surviving *Ocean* snotties Dunovan, Cameron and Price left us to join *Exmouth*.

W/T signal stating that there are at least two hostile submarines in the Aegean. There were known to have been two German and two Austrian submarines here but one blew up on a mine at the Narrows and the other was badly damaged and is being repaired.

At the Dardanelles the Turks are reported to have mounted four light guns from *Goeben* on the Asiatic shore and have shelled 'V' Beach severely from these positions; together with the heavy guns on the Gallipoli shore 'V' Beach is now nearly evacuated. Our wounded brought in here often number 200 a day when there is no attack: these were previously in the Rest Camps which now get 'Jack Johnsons' at them all day long.

Fleet sweepers and destroyers, also trawlers, are doing all the work now between here and Gallipoli. A few days ago ammunition on Gallipoli was reported to be so scarce that on a certain day it was limited to two rounds per gun during a whole 24 hours.

TEN: MILITARY FRUSTRATION ON GALLIPOLI

FRIDAY JUNE 25TH. *Lord Nelson* left during the forenoon escorted by six destroyers to bombard Chanak, with the object of setting it ablaze. They certainly succeeded, as the subsequent bonfire even beat the one caused by Sampson's bombs. She fired 55 shells with the balloon-ship *Manica* spotting.

Played for officers-v.-ship's company at water polo which the latter won by 2-1.

SATURDAY JUNE 26TH. At half an hour's notice again so had to spend a dull day aboard. Several Greek schooners have been seized and brought in recently by our cruisers and boarding steamers in charge of a midshipman.

In the forenoon we had a terrible scare — at least for me — smoke was coming out of the hatch of P 1 turret which naturally gave one the idea the magazine was ablaze and the ship about to blow up — not a pleasant thought after the *Bulwark* disaster. In spite of all precautions taken by the stokers in standing by to pump, the smoke was discovered to be coming from some smouldering waste in the trunk!

SUNDAY JUNE 27TH. *Minerva* arrived early, with German woman spy disguised as a hospital nurse found on board an Italian steamer! (We heard later that she was Austrian and quite easy on the eye. Her passage under naval custody turned out to have been quite agreeable for both captors and prisoner.)

During the forenoon hostile submarine was repeatedly being sighted off the entrance of the harbour so armed drifters were sent out and the gate closed.

We sent a working party of 70 men to fill up the old Italian steamer *Peloro* to be sunk with other steamers of a similar class to form a safe harbour at Kephalo: we carry on with this job every day we are not at half an hour's notice.

Glory arrived during the afternoon having come from Halifax after patrolling off the American coast. *Vengeance* left squadron for Gib. to pay off. Dined in *Lord Nelson* with Lord Graham (our 'Term lieutenant' of Dartmouth days).

MONDAY JUNE 28TH. During the forenoon came good news that our troops had made an advance. The attack of the 29th Division this morning and of the Indian brigade was quite successful. The objective was easily gained. Attack was preceded by a very heavy bombardment by all guns on the Peninsula assisted by ships. Counter-attack at night.

Went ashore at 3.30 and had very enjoyable bathe on a decent sandy beach.

During the forenoon *Euryalus* arrived from Mitylene where they have been harassing enemy submarine bases. They lost one picket-boat by having to abandon her when run aground on Turkish territory under heavy fire.

7 p.m. Yacht *Triad* arrived flying the flag of Vice-Admiral de Robeck at the main.

TUESDAY JUNE 29TH. The Admiral shifted his flag to *Lord Nelson* but transferred it again later when he sailed in *Triad*. Fluter went over to call during the forenoon and came back full of news about how we are going to be anchored off Seddul Bahr surrounded by nets moored to lighters anchored all round us. Apparently not only are we to get shelled from Achi Baba and Asiatic shore, but also we are to be 'fished' by submarines, so we now have in mind the old gladiator's saying 'Make merry tonight for tomorrow we die'.

Many wounded have come in during the day after yesterday's fighting. Also many Turkish prisoners who are mostly old farmer chaps who do a fortnight's training.

It came on to blow and rain hard during the night accompanied by a thunderstorm.

WEDNESDAY JUNE 30TH. *Cornwall* arrived from Mitylene having been looking for enemy submarine bases etc.

Went ashore at 3.30 in the cutter for bathing and there we met the *Prince George* party, who have taken on our job of filling the 'breakwater steamer' by an ingenious overhead trolley wire system.

We have now started on the new net-defence job for protecting our ship at Seddul Bahr. About 20 lighters lie alongside the ship (half a dozen at a time) and the carpenters repair them by stopping leaks and then fit sloping boards to the bulwarks to carry the nets. This is to form the zeriba round us when permanently moored as a floating fortress.

It is reported by secret intelligence that the Turks' morale is now very bad and a lot of the troops had to be shifted. They called Gallipoli the slaughter house. Twenty Turks are said to have been shot in Constantinople the other day for being in a plot to kill some German officers. (We have had similar reports before which we treat with some scepticism.)

THURSDAY JULY 1ST. Many wounded still arriving from Gallipoli, in greater numbers than usual. More reinforcements also are still arriving from England, about 60,000 being reported on their way out.

At 7 p.m. *Venerable* left so as to be in position for bombarding by 5 a.m. tomorrow. *Chatham* and *Kléber* also left, apparently for the same purpose.

FRIDAY JULY 2ND. *Venerable*, *Kléber* and *Chatham* returned, latter left again later. *Canopus* arrived from Malta. We are at half an hour's notice today.

After Gen. Quarters in the forenoon we heard that crew of the repair-ship *Reliance* had mutinied, so sent over guard of 34 marines, who brought aboard the mutineers and they were all fallen in on the quarterdeck divided batches of (1) the arch villains (2) and (3) merely the villains. They must have been very much impressed with our red-tape nonsense, which went on for half an hour. They were then put under guard in the cell flat and coal-bay alley.

Royal George arrived with 5,000 troops whom we landed throughout the night, so that wounded can be sent back to Malta in the same ship.

SATURDAY JULY 3RD. Reported from Gallipoli that during the forenoon 700 'Jack Johnsons' were dropped on 'W' Beach and 800 on 'V' doing little damage, as no gear is now kept on these beaches. General Sir Ian Hamilton reports that since June 28th to last night the Turks have suffered 5,105 killed and 1,500 wounded. We also captured 516 rifles and 126,400 rounds of ammunition.

SUNDAY JULY 4TH. Sunday divisions and church. Went ashore for picnic in the afternoon.

At 3 p.m. we received urgent signals from a Gallipoli beach about hostile submarine, which very shortly afterwards torpedoed the French ammunition and supply ship *Carthage* at anchor, from a range of 5,000 yds. Ship went straight down by the stern with her bows towering up in the air. Sixty-six crew were saved and six were lost.

Big Turkish attack expected tomorrow morning. All their warships are getting in supporting positions and further instructions have been issued to our patrol in the Straits.

MONDAY JULY 5TH. Turks started their very fierce attack on our positions early at daybreak. Aided by their ships they fired over 5,000 shells, but, according to reports, their attack was repulsed with heavy loss to the enemy.

TUESDAY JULY 6TH. I took seamen away under sail in the cutter and did a duty trip, otherwise no activity.

WEDNESDAY JULY 7TH. Ships that are doing all the work to and from the Gallipoli peninsula: all the 24 destroyers: *Basilisk, Beagle, Bulldog, Chelmer, Colne, Foxhound, Grampus, Grasshopper, Harpy, Jed, Kennet, Mosquito, Pincher, Racoon, Rattlesnake, Renard, Ribble* (at Malta), *Savage, Scorpion, Scourge, Usk, Wear, Welland, Wolverine.*

Fleet minesweepers: *Clacton, Folkestone, Gazelle, Hythe, Lynn, Newmarket, Reindeer, Whitby Abbey.*

Trawlers, drifters (or ketches) and a few armed boarding steamers.

THURSDAY JULY 8TH. At 5 a.m. started coaling ship, taking in 422 tons, finishing at 9 a.m. without any breakfast hour.

Picnic in afternoon, spent four hours in water mostly swimming underwater; result, a headache.

Enemy submarines are continually showing their presence off Gallipoli and drifters frequently report some indicator nets missing when gathering them in.

FRIDAY JULY 9TH. 5.30 a.m. *Venerable* sailed with balloon spotting from *Hector*, but they gave away their position to the Turks by passing east of Imbros. Wind proved too much for the balloon so they returned at 6 p.m.

SATURDAY JULY 10TH. We are to make a sortie to Gaba Tepe to bombard enemy positions. Before sailing we saw *Aquitania* arrive with 6,000 of Kitchener's army.

At 10 a.m., having furled nets, we weighed anchor and proceeded out of harbour at 15 knots escorted by two destroyers. We passed east of Imbros and at Kephalo we were met by eight destroyers and a dozen drifters, latter carrying a big, mesh wire net which they laid the seaward side of us when we got in position off Anzac, about 1½ miles from us. Six destroyers then patrolled the shoreward side of us while the others kept a look-out for submarines to seaward with the drifters. An aeroplane went up to look out for submarines, but had to come down again owing to engine trouble. *Manica*'s balloon could not spot for us on account of the wind.

At 2.50 p.m. we dropped a mark-buoy and sounded off Action: I had not even got inside the after turret when they fired a 6-in. at us 200 yds short in line with our stern, but I could not hear it ricochet over us. We opened fire with the fore turret, firing one gun at a time at regular intervals. They continued firing at us with 5.9-in. and 14-in. shell and shrapnel. Foretop was too dangerous and was therefore abandoned, so firing was carried out in local control. Their firing was pretty accurate, at least shots were close to the ship, but as we were stationary they should have had more hits. At 3.30 the after turret opened fire range 10,000 yds and S 3 later, local control. We could easily feel the bumps as they hit us, about 10 times in all, four on armour. Worst hit was at 3.10 when 5.9-in. shell went through wardroom skylight hatch (a good ¾-in. steel) and burst in wardroom making four holes in the deck and even punctured deck in gunroom, besides wrecking wardroom again. Of the other hits, three were on the fore bridge and two in the ship's side forward.

At 4.30 p.m. ceased firing, having fired 96 12-in. full charge, 50 9.2-in. full charge. We observed 10 hits very close to the right gun, which obviously must be knocked out, and five very close to left gun which must at any rate be temporarily knocked out. These are very likely two of *Goeben*'s 5.9-in. guns. At 4.30 we proceeded at 15 knots again and, zigzagging, were escorted by six destroyers as far as Kephalo, when we steadied on Mudros, escorted by two destroyers. At 6 we suddenly sighted an object making a wake like a submarine on the port bow about 3 cables off. Had old Fluter up on the bridge at the run, and just going to alter course when it turned out to be the wash of a drifter's buoy. We arrived at Mudros at 8.15 p.m. and came to anchor, getting out our nets.

Following signals were exchanged. To *Agamemnon*: 'Many thanks and congratulations for excellent shelling on Saturday. I am sure you did much material and moral damage which all here much appreciate. Birdwood.' Reply from Capt. Fyler, *Agamemnon*: 'Your kind message is much appreciated. We are all very pleased to know we have been of service to you and your army, and hope we shall be given another opportunity of repeating it.'

SUNDAY JULY 11TH. This was to be a day for testing net

defences. During the forenoon two rows of lighters with nets attached either side were anchored in line abreast 1,000 yds from the ship. Destroyer *Scourge* then took up position 1,000 yds from nets and fired 21-in. torpedo with 'Pioneer' net-cutter attached. Torpedo failed to penetrate first net (*Prince George*'s old nets) and the 'Pioneer' jammed. The same experiment was carried out in the afternoon in the presence of Captain commanding destroyer flotillas. Torpedo went through first net when it brought up against the 2nd net which it failed to pass through, the head being jammed in the hole. 'Pioneer' jammed again. Hopeless.

Ship's company started aquatic sports in the Dog Watches.

MONDAY JULY 12TH. Spent all forenoon in picket boat unloading *Aquitania*. Two more liners came in full of troops, all Kitchener's army.

In the forenoon the new monitor *Abercrombie* crept into Mudros.

This unusual monster, mounting a turret of twin 14-in. guns, was able to steam only at 6-7 knots and had had to be towed much of her voyage out from England. We learnt that she was 90 ft broad because of her bulges which protruded each side: compartments were of water/air/water, so that should she be torpedoed only the bulge would bear the damage and the actual hull of the ship would not suffer. Her guns, handed over from a continental firm building a battleship for Greece, had an accurate range of 20,000 yds, but by listing the ship she could fire 28,000 yds.

Theseus also came in and like the remainder of the 'Edgar'-class cruisers has cofferdams, fitted for protection against torpedoes, which have not yet been tested. Speed is reduced to 10 knots by this encumbrance. *Prince George* returned in the evening having fired 50 12-in. and a few hundred 6-in. She was hit four times.

TUESDAY JULY 13TH. *Abercrombie* left early for Kephalo to relieve *Chatham*.

A jolly fine sailing breeze and I had a good many trips in the cutter with the sailors.

It was the cutters which provided keen competition between one battleship's midshipmen and those of another. The time was taken from the word 'Go' to set up masts and make sail, to 'shorten sail', 'Out oars and pull'.

A large number of motor lighters are now out here or on their way. They were towed out from England by steamers and are to be used for the new landing of which we know nothing except that a few lighters are fitted with a Bolinder's heavy oil engine driving them at 6 knots or less when filled with 250 men. They have a draught of 4½ ft and forward a ramp lowered by a purchase, and as they draw less than a foot forward they can be run up on a beach. There are hatches all along the top of the lighter which can be lifted up when necessary for a quick disembarkation over the forebrow; at the same time when being taken inshore the men have safe protection against shrapnel and rifle fire.

WEDNESDAY JULY 14TH. All ships hoisted the Allied ensign in honour of the fall of the Bastille. Another nice sailing breeze but no opportunity to make use of it.

THURSDAY JULY 15TH. (*Our harbour life for the next few weeks was especially dull. I have therefore summarised from my diary the insignificant events of the next 10 days.*)

Our ship's company was largely employed in coaling large transports, which continued to arrive with troops. The giant Cunarders *Aquitania* and *Mauretania* demanded far more coal than we could put into them and usually we could provide enough only to enable them to reach Genoa where modern facilities allowed them to complete their bunkers.

I was often busy running the picket-boat, Watch-keeping and being involved with a certain amount of instruction.

To patrol the sea routes and examine shipping we now had steamers, formerly employed on Channel Islands service, Irish mailboats and Isle of Man: *Carron*, *Rowan*, *Sarnia*, *Snaefell*, *Fauvette*, *Heroic* and *Partridge* — now called 'armed boarding steamers'. They boarded neutral steamers and even sailing caiques, and sent them to Mudros (sometimes commanded by a midshipman) for examination, much to the irritation of the Greeks, who were still neutral.

Our submarines, operating in the Sea of Marmara, were as active as ever, sinking Turkish supply and ammunition ships. Monitors, large and small, continued to arrive from England as well as the old cruisers with their hideous cofferdams fitted to their sides.

MONDAY JULY 26TH. Cruiser *Chatham* arrived 8 a.m., bringing out — it was rumoured — Churchill, but it turned out to be Colonel Hankey, Secretary to the War Cabinet.

Important W/T signals from V. A. to Naval Transport officer: 'Provide for nights of 28th, 29th and 30th: three destroyers, two armed boarding steamers, and eight ketches to be kept working all night, arranging reliefs, in disembarking troops from C. Helles to Mudros and Kephalo.'

TUESDAY JULY 27TH. All officers forbidden by Fluter to

discuss any operation taking or going to take place out here; especially the new landing. (Order is from the Admiral.) The old cruisers *Edgar* and *Grafton* arrived during forenoon and like their sisters are fitted with cofferdams which make them look a real picture of ugliness. Hospital yacht *Liberty* (Lord Tredegar) arrived.

Hostile submarine reported aground near De Totts but in spite of our drifters and aeroplanes immediately hurrying to the spot she managed to escape. Another enemy submarine reported off Anzac.

WEDNESDAY JULY 28TH. Hun airman came over here at 5.45 and apparently was not sighted till nearly here. Anyhow he only dropped one bomb which fell near the wireless station, and then made off without being interfered with. Yacht *Beryl* arrived at noon with Admiral Gamble aboard.

Four thousand troops left in transport for Mitylene. The Admiral has also been down there in *Chatham* as well as *Euryalus* and *Canopus*, who have been there some time. They are apparently making preparations for a landing or else it is a pretty good feint. The 29th division are now returning to the Peninsula after a three-week rest. Achi Baba got another fierce bombardment today.

We have now got *K 6* and *K 7* motor lighters ready for the landing, i.e. engines well overhauled and wheelhouse well protected by sandbags.

THURSDAY JULY 29TH. Disembarkation of troops from destroyers returning from the Peninsula began at 5 a.m.

First Lord of Admiralty and Lord Kitchener announce casualties up to July 28th as follows:

Naval 9,106, Military 321,889

Dardanelles: 567 officers, 7,567 men *killed*
Total: 2,144 officers, 47,094 men *casualties*

Agamemnon at half an hour's notice, so played the boys water polo and beat them 5-0, after a pretty good walkover; Anderson scored two goals and I got three.

Picket-boat is once more ready for landing troops and has armoured screen fitted over steering position.

FRIDAY JULY 30TH. More troops brought in again during night. One of our marines, who went mad yesterday, died this morning.

Symonds-Taylor in picket-boat fished up a corpse near the ship, which was a British tommy, who had been foully murdered by having his throat cut and then wrapped up in barbed wire with a 1 cwt sinker which was lifted off the bottom. When the parson went away to bury him properly it took pretty nearly 2 cwt to sink him! After corpse had been removed we played the wardroom water polo and beat them 2-1, which was a very successful result for us.

SATURDAY JULY 31ST. Spent the day in picket-boat disembarking troops from destroyers from 1.30 to 4 a.m.

Hun airman made attack on Tenedos aerodrome but two of our machines went up and brought him down just on the Asiatic shore in square 167 A, so he escaped.

At 7 p.m. five lighters left for Kephalo but it came on to blow during the night and so passage was abandoned. They are so unseaworthy and must return.

Very good polo match, officers v. ship's company which we drew 2-2, self getting both goals by good stroke of luck.

SUNDAY AUGUST 1ST. Picket-boat ordered to be ready to

leave for Kephalo at 8 a.m. tomorrow, so we had a grand draw in which I had the good luck to win, so I made the necessary preparations for a week or two weeks' landing campaign somewhere on Gallipoli.

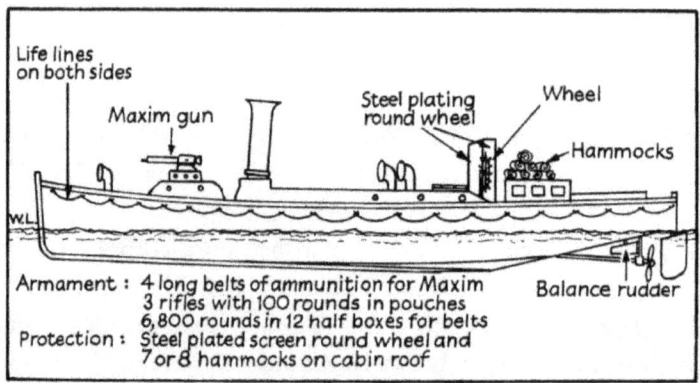

Agamemnon's picket-boat on leaving for Sulva Bay landing. She was the last 56-footer ever built

ELEVEN: NEW LANDINGS AT SUVLA BAY

MONDAY AUGUST 2ND. At 8.30a.m. I left the ship in my picket-boat for trawler 306 to be our escort, lying off *Europa*. I took with me in the boat, in addition to our armament, my hand-bag, basket of rations and good supply of beer. My crew: P.O. Barlow, L.S. Faithful, A.B.s Rising, Shaw, and Macguire; stoker P.O. Langley and stoker Cole.

When the six picket-boats and two steam-pinnaces were ready, trawler weighed and proceeded while squadron formed two divisions in line-ahead formation, pinnaces leading each line while self and *Cornwall*, being fastest boats, were last in each division. Distance between boats half a cable. Pinnaces took station half a cable off trawler's quarters.

As this is the first long voyage I have made by myself, or rather in my own boat, I am quoting everything from boat's log: Mudros to Kephalo 65 miles. Left harbour in forementioned organisation at 10 a.m. Outside boom at 10.30, and gradually felt the lop as we got out to the headland. Wind north, Force 5-6. At 4.30 *Glory*'s steam-pinnace dropped astern of station, remainder proceeded on, but *Cornwall* and *Agamemnon* reduced speed to stand by steam-pinnace. 'Flag' then semaphored to trawler 'Ease down'. At noon we were in open sea, battened down and taking it in green over the bows, so speed had to be further reduced. Shaped course for south of Imbros to get a lee at 1 p.m. Speed was further reduced on account of pinnaces dropping astern and shipping a lot of water; formation was consequently badly kept till 3.30 p.m., when we were in the lee of Imbros and original formation was resumed. 4.30. *Glory*'s pinnace dropped astern, shipped a lot of water in her forepeak and got down by the bows. Squadron stopped to allow her to bale out and catch up. At 6.30 having rounded extreme northern end of Kephalo's indicator nets, trawler left us and squadron formed single line ahead and at reduced speed entered the gate.

At 7.30 I reported to *Exmouth* and was ordered to proceed to monitor *Lord Raglan* and take in coal, water and provisions. I got quite a decent dinner there and damn well wanted it too. At 9.30 we went to the inner harbour and moved up alongside a motor-lighter for the night. *Manica* (balloon ship) arrived at 8 p.m. after spotting for the big monitors. I saw them practising the landing of troops from motor-lighters when we arrived.

TUESDAY AUGUST 3RD. At Kephalo: had a decent night's sleep till 5 a.m. when I was awakened by swarms of flies and by the shrieks and yells of the Egyptian working party.

Ordered to have steam by 9 a.m., we then had to land a General Gauntlett and his staff from a transport.

At 10.30 a.m. all boats made fast to Greek schooner, let fires die out and then overhauled engines and cleaned out boilers. Spent a peaceful day 'caulking', eating and bathing.

I spent a merry evening dining in *Exmouth*. Got back soon after 10 p.m. to find the boat swarming with rats. First Shaw woke up forward and said a rat was walking over him, then Barlow took it up and said that a rat was trying to bite his toes. After turning out the after cabin in the rat hunt, Barlow suddenly woke up at 1 a.m., made the devil of a row and explained how a rat walked over him.

WEDNESDAY AUGUST 4TH. At anchor all day with fires out, hence nothing to do but swim, eat and sleep.

The R.N.R. Lt went to *Havelock* for the night, so made me senior officer of the 12 boats during his absence.

No one has the remotest idea as to where the new landing is to take place and the subject is never brought into conversation in any of the ships I have been to.

THURSDAY AUGUST 5TH. It came on to blow during the night, but I was not told, hence slept through it all. As we were dragging, like everything else, we all raised steam at 8 a.m., for already a couple of motor-lighters were hard aground on a lee shore.

During the forenoon we had to cart the flag-commander about in the very devil of a sea. A description of him and his manners I shall not furnish.

At 4 p.m., I towed out *K 3* lighter to *Osmanieh*, full of Gurkhas, there being such a sea that she could not keep bows onto the waves. We then went to monitor *Raglan* to coal, water and provision. We were told off for duty as Admiral's barge, and later I dined with Rear-Admiral Christian, who dropped a few hints about the new landing, of which he is in charge. Had a decent comfortable night's sleep in *Jonquil*, while my picket-boat got a rotten time moored up astern, in the heavy sea still running.

Realising that our white uniforms would be very conspicuous in the dark, some of us had hastily obtained from one of the ships a quantity of coffee with which we dyed our Whites a sort of khaki colour. This was, after all, more in line with the army and would be far less conspicuous in the darkness.

On August 6th I noted that our troops were all wearing white armbands, evidently to distinguish friend from foe. Some of their officers, I remember talking to late that afternoon, seemed to have no idea where they were to be landed nor the nature of the terrain, although we had a premonition that we would make our landing this very night.

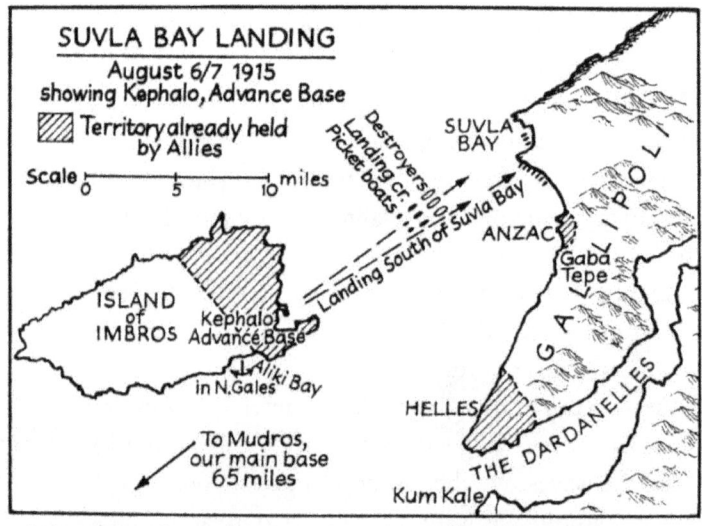

Sulva Bay prior to landing. August 6th/7th 1915, showing Kephalo, advance base

FRIDAY AUGUST 6TH. The night of our landing at Suvla Bay. Spent most of day taking Admiral Christian about the harbour and taking urgent letters from *Triad*, *Ark Royal*, etc., which kept us pretty busy. At 3 p.m. we were relieved and went to *Exmouth* to coal, water and provision; there I learned quite unofficially that the landing, which is taking place tonight, is to be at and near Suvla Bay. All the monitors are out today and, judging by the sound of heavy gunfire, must be heavily engaged.

By 3 p.m. ten of the 'Beagle' destroyers were anchored single line abreast, lying to a north wind. An hour later the ten motor-lighters started filling up with 500 soldiers each and I ferried them to their respective destroyers which were anchored in numerical order from *K 1* to *K 10*. As soon as the destroyers had embarked the lighters' first loads, the latter filled up with another 500 and then made fast alongside their respective destroyers.

When I had finished coaling and watering I shoved off at 4 p.m. and, fortunately, was met by another boat out of which emerged Lt 'Conkey' Hammet (from now on referred to by nickname), who jumped into my boat. We then pushed off to *K 3* and there he explained to me the orders, which were roughly these: *Beagle, Bulldog* and *Grampus*, three motor-lighters and three picket-boats (including us, of course) were to land 3,000 of Kitchener's army at Suvla Bay ('A' Beach) and the remaining seven destroyers, etc., were to land on the beach the other side of Niebruniessi Point ('B' landing).

The three destroyers were to arrive at Suvla Bay about 11 p.m. and then, when the lighters were to go in, it was the duty of the picket-boats to help and stand by them. Also, we learnt that there is to be a grand attack on Achi Baba and another, by the Australians, at Gaba Tepe. There is also to be a feint landing by the volunteer Greeks up the Gulf of Xeros at Bulair, in charge of *Minerva* and *Jed*.

The object of our big landing is to rush the 10,000 men we are to put ashore at Suvla about 8 miles inland during the night and morning, and then be reinforced early next day. Once the bridgehead is held and guns brought up we could command all the supplies going to Achi Baba and so make the entire army at Achi Baba surrender.

Thus it was that at 7.30 p.m., having had some tea, we joined our three destroyers, together with landing craft and picket-boat; weighed and proceeded at about 10 knots out of Kephalo, being cheered by all other transports, etc. There was a strong northerly wind blowing and soon we had to ease down. At 7.30 p.m. we had our supper — sardines with bread and butter and peaches — but Conkey would allow no beer until the morrow. What a damned dull voyage it was, pitch black; we tried to talk all the time but conversation ran out and by nine o'clock we did nothing except smoke pipes and admire the night attack, shells bursting, star shells, etc., and one of us would remark occasionally, 'Oh what a pretty light', or something equally footling. Conkey kept on humming tunes and I occasionally did the same. Although it was dull, I think both of us were in jolly good spirits about our adventure — if it was to be one — except once when Conkey told me he had brought some opium pills. What a damned long passage it seemed.

About 11 o'clock we got close in to the shore at Suvla and soon the three destroyers came to anchor, making the devil of a noise as only one of them muffled her cable. Motor-lighters immediately proceeded in straight ahead of them, while we slipped and, myself taking the wheel, closely followed in the wake of the lighter.

Everything seemed absolutely quiet and, except for a long ground-swell, everything seemed still. The land lay close on our starb. hand and at one time we made out a light ashore as we got further in; we were closing the land on our starb. hand and when about half-way inside the bay, I should estimate the low cliff was then about 500 yds off. Up to this point, I thought we were going to have no opposition; Conkey was standing amidships talking to one of the bowmen about soundings and I was standing up steering with my feet.

Suddenly, I distinctly heard a sharp click ashore, which must have been the cocking of rifles, for only a few seconds later there was one shot followed by hundreds, rapid independent.

Conkey and I got inside our 'wheelhouse' while the boat's crew lay down as best they could on the lee side of the firing. I must say it surprised me a bit to begin with, but what annoyed me most was the devil of a row they made, being so close. Conkey and I had to yell at one another, although only a foot apart.

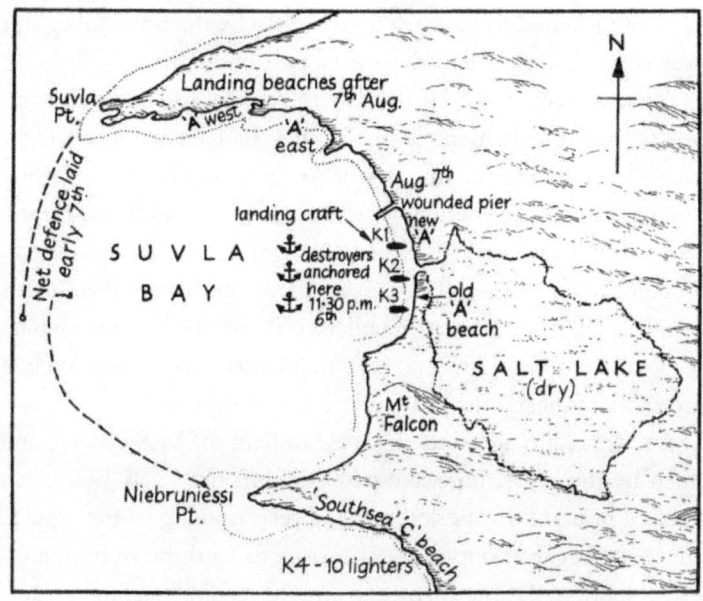

Landing at Sulva Bay on night of August 6th/7th

It was after 11.30 when the lighter grounded in 3 ft of water and in a few minutes troops started to wade ashore above their waists in water. We got a grass line from our stern to the lighter's stern and, by occasionally going ahead, kept her bows on to the beach. In doing this we got stern on to rifle-fire, which went on for a couple of hours pretty well as strong as ever; hence myself and Conkey — especially myself — put great faith in a pile of hammocks on the cabin roof which at least protected our backs and stopped many bullets too! As the lighter emptied, she put her bows further up towards the beach, but in doing so gradually wedged herself between the shore and a reef which projected out from the corner of the bay. I might add that the soldiers were naturally not too keen to get ashore and especially at the end, it took quite a lot of persuasion from the sergeants to clear the lighter. Then the ammunition had to be carried ashore, so by the time the lighter was cleared, it must have been well past midnight.

What a relief it was to hear them say she was cleared, both for us and the lighter coxswain; they had hit us about eight times by counting the number of thuds on the boat and feeling the hammocks jar every time when one went into them. Nearly every shot they fired hit either our lighter or *K 2* (next to us), but generally ours and every hit made the devil of a lot of sparks. Then we got two bullets on our steel screen which almost went through the 1/8-in. plating, and made such a noise that it nearly drove in the drums of my ears.

We were hard aground and tried to haul off by the stern, and then by the bows, but we could not shift her at all. For about half an hour, at this period, we had seen nothing of the crew at all so we began shouting for someone to tend the stern line; all of a sudden Barlow's voice from the cabin, making a great pandemonium, called; 'I've got a wounded man down here. I'm doing my best.' Naturally we expected the whole place to be running in blood but later we found it was only a head wound in A.B. Rising.

After shoving our bows on the reef a good number of times, we now found ourselves hard and fast, and could not budge by engine-power, even helped by hauling on the grass-line. We came to the conclusion that the only other means of getting off was to get out and shove. Thereupon Conkey insisted on getting overboard, and, by means of shoving, we got off, but crashed into the landing craft before we could stop engines; also we took about 10 turns of grass-line round our propeller. Then Conkey waded about on the reef for about 10 minutes, being potted at all the time, and surveyed a channel through the reef. The grass-line being round the screw, he then tried to cut it away, but had to give up, as he got so cold and tired.

Then I went in, taking off my coat but forgetting my wristwatch, and performed underwater operations, staying down for 30 seconds at a time and always cutting at the same strand. I know I imagined I could see by my luminous watch, but I am not absolutely certain now whether I could or not! After about 10 or 15 minutes I had cleared away all the grass-line from the screw and I was not sorry when we let go the lighter and, proceeding very slowly, felt our way through the channel. This was slightly after 1 a.m.; Conkey and I both shifted into dry gear and, groping in the darkness, searched for *Beagle*, where eventually we reported what had happened to our lighter. We were then told to look for a ketch (small type of trawler), with a tow of boats, which we eventually found; after transferring our wounded A.B. Rising we tried to pilot the ketch to the beach, which we found after much difficulty and getting sniped at en route.

The four boats (launch and three lifeboats) were then filled up with troops at *Beagle*, and we towed them in as far as we could to *K 1* lighter which was hard and fast near *K 2*. Another picket-boat was helping and between us, after making about three trips to the beach, we took in the last lot of soldiers just before dawn. After we had left our lighter, we still had all the spent bullets coming at us or past us, but, of course, no one worries much about them.

During the night in Suvla Bay *K 2* lighter remained hard and fast like ours, and *K 1* was the only one that got off after the first load had disembarked. About 100 men in her never went ashore and could not be seen owing to darkness. She proceeded to empty the troops from *Grampus* and also took a few soldiers off *Beagle* and *Bulldog* before going in again; they say she had nearly 700 aboard her last trip ashore.

The seven destroyers for B-landing had arrived at 'B' Beach (S. of Niebruniessi Pt.) and there they landed with no opposition; also being a 'Southsea beach', lighters got right into the shore without difficulty.

The moon rose at 2.30 a.m.; till then a destroyer played her searchlight on 'Chocolate Hill' in order that the soldiers might make for it.

During the night at 'A' and 'B', 10,000 men were landed and then the old cruisers *Theseus* and *Endymion*, which arrived full of troops, landed some in motor-lighters over stern ladders specially constructed.

SATURDAY AUGUST 7TH. Just after dawn we went back to our motor-lighter and tried for nearly an hour to get her off, but it was no good. A sniper or two potted at us all this time and although never more than 200 yds from the boat, he did not hit us. At early dawn I could see only a few soldiers meandering quite unmolested along the shore. Quite extraordinary.

We then proceeded out and found Commander Unwin who did not immediately require us, so we were not sorry to get something to eat and, more especially, to drink. Meanwhile just after dawn, *Rowan*, *Sarnia* and three other armed boarding steamers came to anchor close to northern shore of bay and disembarked troops in lighters to that shore without opposition. These steamers, however, got shelled rather badly (*Sarnia* got hit) and consequently had to shift billet out of it.

At 5 a.m. a lot of other ships had arrived and they all took up their billets quickly and came to anchor. Ships were *Jonquil* (flag R. A. Christian), *Aster, Talbot, Chatham*, two small monitors, six transports and a couple of colliers. *Queen Victoria*, steaming 10 knots, then laid the anti-submarine net round the Bay. As soon as *Talbot* arrived she started firing salvoes, trying to support our troops, who were having a grand attack and were advancing on the flanks, but centre was held up.

Apparently, as we felt at the time and learnt later, our men should have pushed on much more vigorously as there were barely three or four battalions of Turks up against them when the order was given to dig in. We heard a few days afterwards that General Stopford, in charge of the whole landing, was relieved, and sent home to England. We suffered a lot of casualties at this time owing to their heavy shrapnel fire on our reserves at Mt. Falcon, who then took cover and dug in.

Soon after 6 a.m. we were told by *Jonquil* to take in boats to the north side of the Bay and make a start getting off the wounded; we went on with this till 3 p.m., when we returned to *Jonquil* to coal and water — usually taking about 12 cwt of coal.

During the day there was a strong breeze from the north which made this job rather difficult, especially as hospital-ship *Soudan* was anchored right out at sea. At noon a Taube was right over us when we were out at the hospital ships, and our friend Fritz dropped two bombs not more than a couple of hundred yards from either hospital-ship (and us of course!).

By the afternoon 15,000 reinforcements had been landed at 'C' Beach and at New 'A' Beach on the north side of Bay; there was not much fighting during the day except for a few shells on 'C' Beach, when everyone bolted for the Red Cross flag.

Owing to heavy shrapnel on Lala Baba, reinforcements all dug in.

At 5 p.m. we were ordered to go to *Minneapolis* to bring off Australian pier party to construct a pontoon pier. We took this pier party into New 'A' Beach and then went ashore with Captain of *Jonquil*; Conkey and I had a good look round, seeing plenty of dead Turks and nearly getting blown up by a mine.

On the beach we met an old General of '50 something' who had lost his staff and had also been drenched and wanted to get to the transport *Minneapolis* for some dry gear; so we said we would take him as he seemed so cheery about it. We first shifted pontoon pier further along into next cove and were going astern to get clear of the shore in about 3 fathoms of water when suddenly our stern shot right out of the water on a submerged rock. After I had shocked the old General by most unparliamentary language we found we were minus the rudder and part of the screw so we had in future to steer with 'balance rudder', which was very dangerous, especially with boats in tow. We then proceeded to *Jonquil* and got some dinner there and, feeling absolutely dead, I turned in in the picket-boat at 9 p.m.; this was after listening to a great strafe about embarking the wounded, between the Admiral's flag-captain and Rear-Admiral Christian's flag-lieutenant.

Apparently our picket-boat was ordered away at 10 p.m. and old Conkey carried on with wounded till 2 a.m. in the devil of a sea; but he said absolutely nothing would wake me and I slept on like a log till dawn.

Meanwhile *Soudan* sailed in the evening and *Valdivia* is now being filled up with wounded. Some of the transports in harbour here: *Minneapolis, Suevic, Medic, Ulysses, Derfflinger* (prize), *Sudmark* (prize), *Crosshill* and some colliers.

SUNDAY AUGUST 8TH. Started at dawn towing boats of wounded from 'A' Beach and then 'C' Beach, the new beaches on the N. side of the Bay; the original 'A' Beach, being too exposed, was abandoned. Here I had a bathe, just like being at Southsea. *Bacchante* started shelling top of ridge between 'B' Beach and Anzac; big monitors and small ones also occasionally shelling this area.

Wounded ceased to come down at 3.30 so we towed all the boats round to Old 'A' Beach. One of our aeroplanes dropped a message at 'B' saying that the Turks were bringing up guns to bombard beach, so everyone there was packing up gear in preparation for the shelling. 5 p.m. Monitor *Havelock* went in close to Old 'A' Beach and started shelling possible gun position on the ridge. It may have done some good, as 'B' did not get shelled that day.

At 7 p.m. we had to land Conkey to regulate boats for wounded, so in future there is no one to talk to and always perpetual watch. I had to go on with wounded in a strong tide and heavy lop till after midnight when we anchored off 'A' Beach. I have reason to believe I drowned a couple of men by allowing one boat to get under the discharge (circulator) of the hospital-ship, nearly filling up the boat as well. The boats with wounded had to lay off the hospital-ship for 8 hours sometimes: it seemed so damned silly sending them out there when they could not be embarked quicker.

Fresh water at Suvla Bay is running very short and all H.M. ships are distilling hard while the merchantmen are having their tanks emptied. Wounded at 'A' are not even getting sufficient water and other troops are doing without it.

Triad arrived at 5 p.m. with the Admiral who signalled: '*E 11* arrived in Sea of Marmara torpedoed gunboat *Berki-Satvet* which was beached, also three big empty transports, and in company with *E 14* together bombarded troops proceeding west along the Bulair-Karac road throughout August 7th. This caused them many casualties.'

MONDAY AUGUST 9TH. At Suvla front there was a general attack by our troops at 3 a.m. In a picket-boat we were much out of touch with the fighting ashore but we heard later that our people got in a fearful mix-up in the dark, German officers giving our troops orders with the result that some were surrounded. All the W. Yorks, except a dozen or two men, reported wiped out altogether, while the Lincolns, on our right, also got fearfully cut up even worse than the Yorks. 5 a.m. Violent bombardment from *Talbot* and *Theseus* firing right over us at the ridge: this was followed by fierce musketry.

Wounded started coming down at 6 a.m. and we soon began taking them off to *Clan MacGillivray*. At 10 a.m. a lot of reinforcements were landed at Niebruniessi Point. Carried on with wounded all day right up to 11.30 p.m., except for coaling and watering, and we filled up both the Clan steamers and *Soudan* with wounded.

At 11.30 p.m. heard a lot of musketry-fire on our left and centre. We anchored off 'A' Beach just before midnight.

TUESDAY AUGUST 10TH. Started before daylight to bring in empty boats from *Soudan*, who immediately sailed. We then went to *Swiftsure* to water and were ordered to tow five lifeboats to our left flank, round Suvla Point, to bring off wounded. Eventually, we found *Grampus* and a trawler about half-way between Arapos and the Kichlar Rocks; the destroyer semaphored to me: 'Wounded will not be down till 1.30 a.m.', so we anchored and sent in the boats to the beach, and took the opportunity to bathe. Meanwhile, at 7 a.m., all ships were supporting our troops along the whole line.

During the forenoon there were only two wounded men whom I sent in the trawler to the hospital-ship, and then we took water ashore from *Grampus* in makeshift tarpaulins. We gave them our own breakers, for they lacked containers.

We anchored again off the west flank near the shore for a while, but a sniper kept potting at us, although *Grampus* occasionally fired at Turkish snipers up on the slope of the hill. Beyond that everything was pretty quiet, the only noise being the rifle-report of the occasional sniper potting at us or at *Grampus*. At 4 p.m. another picket-boat came round and told me to proceed back to *Swiftsure* at once. I arrived there at about 5.15 and made a report to Rear-Admiral Christian about the positions and conditions of our left flank.

During the afternoon the transports *Wiltshire* and the American *Northland* (late *Zealand*) arrived.

By about 5 p.m. the Australian pier-party had completed a pontoon pier at Old 'A' Beach, much simplifying transportation of wounded.

There was no hospital-ship off Suvla all day, and wounded were rapidly accumulating at Old 'A' Beach after this morning's retreat. *Aster* and *Newmarket* were accordingly filled up, or were being filled up, when we got back, so as soon as we had coaled and watered, we went in to help take off wounded to these ships which were lying inside the harbour for a change. Hospital-ship *Clan MacGillivray* arrived again at 7 p.m., but as it was well after 10 p.m. when we had finished with the *Aster* and *Newmarket*, we packed up for the night and anchored off 'A' Beach again.

WEDNESDAY AUGUST 11TH. Started at 5 a.m. taking wounded off to *Clan MacGillivray*. At 5.30, just as we were passing *Chatham* we saw *Havelock* firing a one-pounder pompom at a Taube, which suddenly dropped a bomb very close to the *Chatham* and the other one very near the *Manica* (balloon ship).

Following my instructions I proceeded *to Swiftsure* at 8 a.m. in order for the boat to be ready to proceed to Mudros at noon, for without her proper rudder she was quite unserviceable for hospital-boat towage. I am staying on here to take *Lord Nelson*'s picket-boat.

After a d—d good breakfast I slept like a log till after 4 p.m., when I was informed I should have to shift billet and take my picket-boat to *Euryalus* the next day. (*Euryalus* had arrived from Mitylene in the forenoon.) Submarines *E 2* and *E 14* went alongside *Triad*.

At the New 'A' Beach, we are putting up Red Cross flags everywhere, even where there is not a dressing station and ammunition is all stacked by these flags as well as stores, etc. The Australians are very fed up with us doing such a thing and quite right too.

THURSDAY AUGUST 12TH. Started work at 7 a.m. in *Lord Nelson*'s picket-boat (50 ft) and proceeded to tow water-lighters ashore all the forenoon. The Turks could always spot a water-lighter: a priority target.

At 2 p.m., when I was about to come alongside *Swiftsure*, a small field-gun (12-pdr) had opened fire on her. Just as I got alongside they started hitting her and I was ordered to proceed to sea with this big water-lighter. *Swiftsure* then slipped her stern anchor, weighed her bower and proceeded out to sea. *Cornwall* was also getting straddled, but by working her engines avoided being hit. All merchantmen weighed and some proceeded to sea, but were soon recalled when shelling ceased.

After 40 minutes *Swiftsure* came to anchor again and when I got aboard I found she had been hit 10 times and had had five killed and 10 wounded. *Grafton* off 'C' Beach did worse and had nine killed, 10 wounded.

My night patrol off the Gate from 8 p.m. tonight to daylight. Went dead slow all night across the Gate and occasionally patrolled along the southern section of net. Examined all craft that passed through Gate which were mostly trawlers. *E 2* left at 1 a.m., when I also heard fierce musketry; no doubt our night attack.

FRIDAY AUGUST 13TH. At 5 a.m., being quite light, I returned to *Swiftsure* and had to take Lt Campbell, R.N.R., about the harbour towing lighters, etc., till 8 a.m., when there started a proper 'morning hate', as expected, and all ships had to weigh and work engines. After *Cornwall* had been very nearly hit by big howitzer shells, all ships came to anchor in the same relative positions, but further out nearer the net. At 8 a.m. I was relieved and turned in till 4 p.m., when I was requested to shift my abode to *Euryalus* with half a dozen others. *Venerable*'s boat was already there, so I came back at 10 p.m. and got a 'night in' instead.

Old 'A' Beach got shelled yesterday near the Red Cross flags, but after a time it stopped and a Turk under a white flag came down to apologise for it. As a matter of fact they really have every right to shell it as we use it as a thoroughfare for soldiers, also mules are watered there.

SATURDAY AUGUST 14TH. Started at 4 a.m. running Lt Bernard, R.N.R., about towing lighters, etc.

About noon hostile submarine sighted outside the net, and she fired two torpedoes at *Manica* both of which missed and hit the net at an acute angle and burst. Not much shelling today; I saw only a few big howitzer shells fall on 'A' Beach west, but they do not do much harm in spite of the noise and dust they kick up.

Left ship at 7.30 p.m. with Nichol (sub-Lt) for night patrol in charge of three other boats. The deuce of a rough night and very dark, cold and miserable; we took the northern section of nets which are very irregular and difficult to patrol. I kept the first part of the night till 1 a.m. and during this period the coxswain, who was a young b.f., got hold of the Very pistol which I had already loaded and I'm damned if he did not fire the thing right in front of my face. The fool was so scared he dropped the pistol in the ditch; well, the flash absolutely blinded me, but having told him what I thought of him I was now interrupted at intervals by boats charging up, asking where the submarine was. Now two rockets is the signal, not one. I added that I had a clown in the boat, who chose to sit on a rocket and make it go off. Anyhow, in the pandemonium a trawler got on the net trying to ram the 'submarine' and felt very insulted when told there was not one. The Rear Admiral sent his boat out to investigate, so again I had to explain. Well, I turned out the sub. at 1 a.m. and the next thing I remember was hearing a grating noise, the engine stop and bad language. I soon found we were on the net and this fool of a coxswain was the culprit, as the sub. put him in charge at 4.15 just as it began to get light.

It came on to blow hard and we were riding by our propeller all that forenoon till after midday and the boat took it in by the bucketful over the stern so we had to keep the hand-pumps going all the time. We had no steam as the stoker had let fires die out being almost as incompetent as the coxswain.

SUNDAY AUGUST 15TH. At last a relief crew was sent out at 12.30 and I was not sorry to get back to *Euryalus* soaked to the skin, and get some food and sleep. Eventually at 4 p.m. they sent off divers who cut the wires holding the propeller. I don't know how the boat ever rode to the gale by her screw the way she did, especially when we had the whole weight of a trawler which came to our assistance.

Ships all got shelled at 9 a.m. and had to shift out of it as usual. Ships' guns supported our troops all the afternoon while we are trying to advance on the left. Reinforcements arrived in destroyers.

Heard that *Royal Edward* has been torpedoed off Crete with 1,700 troops aboard. Hospital-ship *Soudan* rescued 400 but was ordered off by submarine.

MONDAY AUGUST 16TH. Turks shelled New 'A' Beach all the forenoon, also 'C' Beach, which, of course, always goes on and all boats going in there get shelled. At 8 a.m. enemy submarine was reported outside off the net, but no fish were seen to be fired. We are now protected by 12 lighters with double rows of nets which we had fitted out at Mudros. I took an afternoon off, it being my night patrol tonight.

At 5 p.m. and 6.15 we were shelled so had to go to Gen. Quarters. At 7 p.m. they again fired on the merchantmen, hitting only one, but they also dropped one through the stern of a trawler carrying ammunition to Anzac. Latter gradually settled down by the stern till only her bows remained vertically up for about 5 minutes. Everyone was saved, including the cat.

Left at 7.30 p.m. for patrol and spent most of the night laying off south buoy making three long flashes while ships came in till 4 a.m. On account of having a b.f. of a coxswain I had to swear I would keep awake all night, before leaving

Euryalus, and by smoking about six pipes was enabled to keep my vow.

TUESDAY AUGUST 17TH. At 4 a.m. we carried on patrolling as the four steamers had now come in. At 6 a.m. I returned to *Euryalus* and had to land troops at New 'A' Beach from armed boarding steamers and destroyers. Returned to *Euryalus* with the intention of getting some sleep, but of course those d—d Turks shelled us at 11 a.m. and 2 p.m., thus disturbing my rest. They are so afraid of piffling little shells in this ship that they go to Gen. Quarters every time.

We had some fun at 5 p.m., when a couple of Taubes were knocking around bombing everything, and one of them made a beeline for *Euryalus*. We had all the marines blazing away with rifles and Maxims; Fritz was very low and I could see his machine very clearly. When he got nearly plumb over us, everyone bolted down below or lay flat and then he dropped a couple of bombs, one 100 yds one side and the other 100 yds t'other.

Signal for all ranks and ratings to rejoin *Agamemnon* and *Lord Nelson*. Everyone did so except a few sailors in lighters, and me.

I have no idea why this order was given. Whether the naval staff wanted us to have a final bash at the Narrows, or did they hear a rumour that Goeben *was to make a sortie and thus they wanted the two strongest battleships in fighting condition to meet her — we never knew.*

WEDNESDAY AUGUST 18TH. During the night 5,000 more troops arrived in *Doris*, fleet sweepers and *Sarnia*; these were landed during early morning and forenoon. At 11 a.m. the ships got shelled, especially the merchantmen, who all had to shift. The Turks did some good practice on *Manitou*, straddling her frequently and hitting her twice. The New 'A' Beach got shelled by big howitzers kicking up a lot of dust, but doing little material damage.

At 6.30 left again for night patrol, having again taken the same vow not to sleep, after a hard day's work (a dirty trick!). Wind blowing from south. At 10 p.m. we picked up a dinghy pulling aimlessly outside the net looking for some merchant steamer. We did them the kindness of allowing them to make fast to us for a few minutes, but then the d—d fools let their painter get round our screw and jammed up the engine; so the officer of the patrol found us drifting helplessly while I was carrying out diving operations. Having just seen a shark before I went in, it was not over pleasant, but I took the precaution of making the crew keep a sharp look-out and also had a line round me. After an hour my efforts met with success. (A number of sharks have been seen recently.)

THURSDAY AUGUST 19TH. Returned to ship at 6 a.m. and then went on landing water in lighters till 8 a.m., when we returned to the ship and I got some sleep.

We got shelled at 1.30 p.m. but I slept on in peace, and they soon stopped it. We got ready for an evening hate but it did not come off.

Water is getting very short on the beach, there being four divisions there now, and it has to be landed all day and night.

My ankles have completely given out now so I get 2 hours' massage at the Sick Bay which seems to do good. More serious, all the men in horse boats are going sick with enteric.

FRIDAY AUGUST 20TH. At 6.50 a.m., just as I was turning out, they started their usual morning hate but nothing much happened.

Reinforcements were landed from *Osmanieh* and another ship of Khedival line; about 2,500 men altogether.

Both Old and New 'A' Beaches got shelled a lot during the forenoon, during which period I looked after troops and water, which is a bit of a change after looking after horse lighters previously.

Left at 6.30 p.m. for night patrol with Senior Officer Lt Adams, R.N.R.; we were able to moor up to North Gate buoy till 11 p.m., when the wind shifted round to the N.E. and we had to lay off.

At 11 p.m. three steamers anchored off 'C' Beach and landed about 2,000 men; they proceeded round to Suvla at daybreak. After midnight fierce musketry going on all along the line; no doubt our big night attack.

SATURDAY AUGUST 21ST. Returned to *Euryalus* at 6 a.m. and had to help land 1,000 men from *Osmanieh* and *Queen Victoria*. We started landing them in flat-bottomed rafts at 'A' east, but then the ships got fired on, as well as us, towing boats in, so had to proceed further out when there was a horrid sea running.

Troops prepared for a general advance during the afternoon so all ships closed right in shore and fired pretty well all the afternoon from 2.30 to 6 p.m., when they again returned to proper billets. Ships shelling were *Euryalus, Swiftsure, Chatham* and *Talbot*. Our shooting was pretty bad; I know for a fact that one casemate had 7 on their fuse instead of 27 and hence wasted shrapnel on our own troops. At about 4 p.m. we got the signal 'Our troops are now in possession of hill 70.'

SUNDAY AUGUST 22ND. Brought a marked change in my duties. Having got absolutely fed up with life out here; i.e., night patrol every other night and all night up with a fool of a coxswain, I have at last obtained permission to return to Mudros in *Lord Nelson*'s boat, but only after worrying the life out of several officers.

Hence at 8.30 a.m. 1 left *Euryalus* in *Lord Nelson*'s boat for trawler 770 and, in company with *Lord Nelson*'s other boat and a steam-pinnace, we left in tow of trawler and shaped a course for Port Mudros. Sea very calm and from N.E. I kept the forenoon and slept the afternoon but at 4 p.m. I found the wind and sea had increased and tow ropes kept parting, even 6-in. grass lines. At 6 p.m. sea got pretty rough, so I decided to slip the trawler and proceeded with other picket boat round the headland and thence for the boom and entrance to Port Mudros, arriving at *Agamemnon* at 7.30 p.m. She has now got her quarterdeck awning spread and I am not sorry to get back to comfort, decent food and plenty of it, iced drinks and plenty of sleep.

TWELVE: TRANSPORT LOSSES AND FRUSTRATION

MONDAY AUGUST 23RD. At Mudros. Back in *Aggie* again.

Since I have been away from the ship, they have had to stop all bathing, as we have now 40 sick with dysentery and a good few ashore with enteric. Everyone has been inoculated against enteric, but still two have already died of it (P.O. Saffil whom we lent to *Rowan* and a private of marines). I got a great fat needle dug into me by Spaldino for my first dose of inoculation.

Total casualties since the landing on August 6th up to the present, including Achi Baba, Anzac and Suvla amount to 37,000; thus bringing up the total out here to 100,000 or more.

TUESDAY AUGUST 24TH. Transport *Manitou* ran aground in West Channel pretty hard and fast lifting up her bows quite a lot. They will probably have to take a lot of gear out of her before they get her off. Later four tugs failed to shift *Manitou* off the mud; she is now disembarking mules, reckoning two to the ton. There are 300 to come out, but even then I expect a lot of coal will have to come out too.

For the next few weeks Agamemnon, *together with other battleships, led an idle life at Mudros. We could not go to help the troops at Gallipoli because of the growing danger of German submarines, and so my diary has dull accounts of transports arriving with still more troops for Gallipoli, our night patrols of the harbour defences, landing ship's company both for route marches and recreation, and my manning the picket-boat.*

We midshipmen found ourselves having to undergo instruction both under the aegis of Schoolie (the instructor officer) and the specialist officers in gunnery, torpedo and navigation. We managed to land for the occasional picnic or for bathing, but on the whole, life took on a boring aspect and was a great contrast to our fighting the Turks.

The ship's company's main recreation was water-polo in which they took as much interest as in football in later years. Every evening there would be two or three matches alongside. We had a successful ship's team in which I was proud to be a member of the forward line.

Our No. 1 picket-boat, once more repaired, was now fitted with a new rudder. The Maxim gun had been removed and a 3-pdr had replaced it; this puts her down by the bow and makes her unseaworthy besides reducing her speed to barely 10 knots. The steel structure round the wheel has been removed. These two 56-ft steam picket-boats were designed for general purposes, such as communication with ship and shore and between one ship and another, as well as towage. They were also mini-warships, being armed with a 3-pdr gun and two 14-in. torpedoes carried in 'dropping gear', mounted one either side, though at Suvla Bay my boat was armed with only a Maxim instead of a 3-pdr. The torpedo armament was effectively used on April 18th by Majestic's *and* Triumph's *picket-boats to blow up our stranded submarine* E 15.

FRIDAY SEPTEMBER 3RD. *Mauretania* arrived with 5,000 troops, all Kitchener's men. She now has a 6-in. gun mounted on her counter and manned by a navy gun's crew, so they think they are now quite safe against submarines, especially with a maximum speed of 25 knots. *Empress of Britain* also arrived full of troops.

Submarine *E 11* arrived from her second cruise in the Sea of Marmara. During her sorties she has torpedoed the battleship *Barbarossa*, one destroyer, 27 steamers, as well as sinking 57 sailing craft with her recently fitted 12-pdr gun. We learnt that on her last trip she had been up there 30 days and was at her last gasp before coming back; lack of fresh water was apparently the greatest worry, for they could obtain no more than what they took with them. Going up and passing through the Narrows they could not get through the net on their first attempt, and it was only by going at it full speed that they managed to get through. They were down at 110 ft when they first struck the net and it brought them up to 90 ft before they got through.

Learning of these difficulties, Fluter had taken it upon himself to design a method of destroying the Turks' anti-submarine net at Nagara. Unfortunately he has seen Commander Nasmith of *E 11* who has told him that if the present net was destroyed they would only put a stronger one in its place.

Most merchant ships and transports were now arriving armed with a gun mounted on the poop. This was sometimes successful in driving off an attacking enemy submarine operating on the surface. One incident was on September 2nd, when urgent signals at 8.30 a.m. from Southland *(late* Vaterland, Antwerp-American line) *stated she had been torpedoed 20 miles south of Mudros. All destroyers and small craft were ordered to proceed to the scene and all the 1,500 soldiers were brought in to Mudros without any casualties. It appears that the submarine fired two fish at her, one of which hit her port side forward and the other passed under her stern. The crew of one of our destroyers manned her and helped bring her in; she arrived at 8 p.m. and was beached to the southward of East Pass. She was fitted with an anti-submarine gun with which she drove off the submarine after the latter had fired her second fish.*

The same day, Ben-my-Chree, *a fast paddler, unarmed, brought in a good many soldiers from Gallipoli. (Sunk later at Kastelorizo.) Erskine Childers, author of* The Riddle of the Sands, *was serving aboard her as lieutenant R.N.V.R.*

On September 8th a submarine was sighted off Strati by Sarnia *who opened fire on her in reply to submarine's fire; the submarine subsequently dived and was not seen again.*

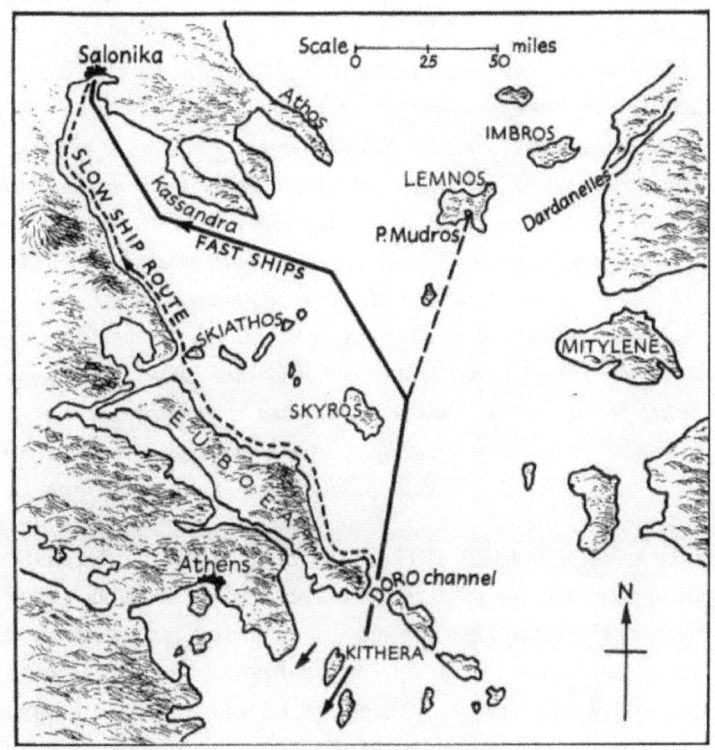

New shipping routes, October 1915: Doro Channel to Salonika

Meanwhile our transport supply problem was becoming acute. German submarines were sinking nearly an average of one ship a day, a good proportion being in our part of the Mediterranean. Even our oldest battleships had had their gun-turrets removed in order to augment the transport of troops from England to the Dardanelles: Hannibal, Mars, Magnificent, *etc. The transports either go to Salonika or must be unloaded at Mudros, and then troops and stores transferred by destroyers, armed boarding steamers, motor-lighters and small craft for conveyance to the improvised harbours of sunken barges, old steamers, etc., off the beaches of Gallipoli.*

We now had anti-submarine patrols right down to Kithera Channel and ships are escorted in relays.

The two transport routes to Salonika operating late in the year were these: 'A route' for fast ships from Doro Channel to 10 miles east of Lithari Point, Skyros Island; on reaching 39th parallel, they proceeded to a point 10 miles north of Plathura Island, thence to a point 10 miles S.W. of Kassandra Point to Cape Kara, where they would be met by guard-boat to pilot them through nets into Salonika. 'B route' for slow ships from Doro Channel to the coast of Euboea keeping in territorial waters passing west of Skiathos Island and creeping up the coast to Salonika. 'B route' is evidently to enable the slow ships to beach themselves if attacked. Vessels for Mudros would branch off at Skyros.

FRIDAY OCTOBER 15TH. At 8.15 a.m. I left in picket-boat from *Roman Prince* to disembark Gurkhas' kit in a big Greek lighter. These Gurkhas hoisted out their own gear working at about ten times the speed of any Englishmen. An English sergeant was in charge of them and he told me they are most excellent workers as well as fighters; discipline is very strict. He said it is very bad for them that white women should make such a fuss of their wounded in England. We also came across Sikhs and Punjabis. We finished work at 3.30 p.m. and I managed to pinch a couple of cartridge-cylinders out of the holds before leaving. We were all mad keen on War trophies!

SATURDAY OCTOBER 16TH. The crew of the transport *Celtic Pride* all got 'bottled' on pilfered whisky and wine, so we took three of them aboard and put them in cells.

Servia has declared war on Bulgaria. The Germans have crossed the Danube into Servia losing 20,000 dead and 40,000 wounded. Both France and Britain are sending troops to the front via Salonika to reinforce the Serbs. Great Britain declared war on Bulgaria at 10 p.m. last night. Our blockade of Bulgarian coast started 6 a.m. this morning, neutral vessels being given two days' grace to clear out.

SUNDAY OCTOBER 17TH. Still sitting in Mudros Harbour providing labour for transports. Everyone is just about fed up with this sort of life, sitting in port like a d—d depot ship, sending away every day big parties of men for coaling, diving, stores, etc.; often 200 men away every day. Why can't the Egyptian labour corps do some of this? We also fit out motor-lighters alongside, overhaul old picket-boats, etc. After four months of this monotonous life it is enough to make anyone fed up, especially after having had only 48 hours' leave in the last 18 months.

MONDAY OCTOBER 18TH. A great catastrophe took place this morning: our jackdaw, while flying round the ship, got blown a long way astern by a great gust of wind. He tried for a long time to fly back, but eventually flopped exhausted into the ditch and unfortunately died before the steam-cutter could get to his rescue.

Perhaps the jackdaw tragedy added to our depression when we thought of how the Suvla Bay battle had been lost within the first few days after our landing. At that time my diary, through lack of opportunity, could not be written up until some days later, and consequently omitted much of what had so much impressed me at the time. I later remembered so vividly my poor impression of the staff on the bridge of the H.Q. ship when I reported on our left Hank, i.e. the limping Gen. Stopford and his too thirsty Chief of Staff, the General we collected ashore who told me he 'had lost his staff', but was making no effort to find them. These and many other incidents came to mind and helped to explain why our troops never got a move on until it was far too late.

At the same time we knew little of what was happening elsewhere: the German pursuit of the Servian army into Macedonia; Bulgaria entering the war on the wrong side; and the confusion of thought among the War Cabinet in London.

TUESDAY OCTOBER 19TH. Concert held on the quarterdeck at 5 p.m., attended by Vice-Admiral Guepratte, which was a great success. At the close of the concert, Fluter made a fairly decent address to Guepratte, to which the latter responded in French, making a very fine and impressive speech about the 'gallant *Agamemnon*' and her fine and praiseworthy actions of the past:

(*In English*) 'I must apologise for not speaking in your beautiful language but I fear I am not sufficiently intimate with it to do so.

(*In French*) 'My friends of *Agamemnon*; I have spent nearly a year in the Dardanelles fleet, a year glorious to our navies, and the whole time has passed like a happy dream. It is the happiest year in my whole naval career and one that will never fade from my memory. It causes me much grief to be leaving it now and parting from my brave men and your splendid soldiers and sailors, especially those of *Agamemnon*.

'Then there is your brave Captain, beside whom I have had the honour of fighting; I shall regret much leaving him. I shall also regret leaving your gallant chief, Vice-Admiral de Robeck, with whom I have been associated in so great a work. The gallant *Agamemnon* is always the same whether in battle or in harbour, it is such a pleasure to come aboard and I have always been treated so cordially. Long live the Royal Navy.

'We are one and always will be. With all my heart I wish you and your splendid country the best of luck in our great and glorious task, and a speedy achievement.

'When I am back and out of the fighting line, I shall always look back here with feelings of happiness and think of all my comrades and watch eagerly for your progress. Good bye.'

The gallant French Admiral was much beloved by us all and he was cheered to the echo!

As the weeks sped by, we snotties had given much speculation among ourselves as to whether the British could hold on to Gallipoli. Transports, despite their losses, kept arriving with fresh troops, a large proportion of which went on to Gallipoli and a few to Salonika where, since October 5th, we had also been sending troops. At the same time many soldiers were brought back to the Mudros field-hospitals suffering from wounds or sickness. As regards progress the fight for Gallipoli had reached a stalemate, for the Turks with German help were becoming stronger. Yet it seemed to us that it would be even more costly in casualties to evacuate than the landing. Our minds were soon to be set at rest.

THIRTEEN: ARRIVAL OF LORD KITCHENER

TUESDAY NOVEMBER 9TH. *Cruiser Chatham* arrived from Marseilles at 8.30 a.m. with Lord Kitchener and staff who were taken to *Lord Nelson*, where in the evening there was a banquet attended by all Generals, our Admiral, and Rear-Admiral Wemyss.

THURSDAY NOVEMBER 11TH. I was sent to attend on *Chatham* at 10 a.m. and landed in my picket-boat General Sir Charles Munro, Sir John Maxwell, Lord Anglesey and staff captain at North Pier. They had arrived on November 8th from Alexandria in the cruiser *Dartmouth*. A few minutes later *Lord Nelson*'s boat brought in Lord Kitchener, General Birdwood and staff, who were received by a large guard and then driven off in eight motor-cars to inspect troops, hospitals and shore installations at Mudros. The following days they were taken to Helles and Anzac. They saw *Royal George* arrive full of troops on Thursday 12th; they learnt of five less fortunate transports; Italian *Ancona* sunk (with only 482 men saved), and British *Mercia*, shelled by submarine en route to Salonika with the loss of 25 killed and 50 wounded.

SUNDAY NOVEMBER 14TH. Lord Kitchener, in spite of heavy weather, sailed for Suvla in destroyer *Laforey* and distinguished himself by being the only General not seasick.

The Turks seem to be getting a lot of war material through from Germany now. New high-explosive ammunition is being used by Turkish howitzers firing at Anzac and now they are reported to have guns on both sides of the Gulf of Xeros, where not long ago there was not a single gun.

The Germans, according to a secret memo in Fluter's cabin, have roughly 30 submarines out here, including the six or eight up in the Sea of Marmara. It is known that four have already been sunk.

Lord Kitchener sailed for home on November 24th having already visited Greece and tried to win over the Greek government to the Allied cause. He then returned to *London overland via Paris, having reached a decision, we hoped, about the future of Gallipoli.*

We now drifted back into the lethargy of being once more a harbour defence ship with as many as 200 men out of the ship every day, usually coaling or unloading transports. The large Cunarders, Aquitania *and* Mauretania, *we were still unable to bunker fast enough for their voyage to England.*

We had a series of gales and blizzards towards the end of the month — that of 29th was probably the worst, with temperature down to zero and serious destruction of temporary breakwaters at all the beaches. It was reported that the keel of the sunken Majestic *had now rolled over and was no longer visible to the soldiers from 'V' Beach, and that* River Clyde[9] *would surely break up.*

---

[9] Actually *River Clyde* survived, was refloated in 1919 and subsequently sold to a Spanish company. She remained in service until 1966 after a life of 61 years.

FOURTEEN: WINTER STORMS AND HEAVY CASUALTIES

Much of our news of conditions on the Peninsula came from newspapers brought out by the mail from England.

The extract below from a report by Ward Price, the Daily Mail's *correspondent, describes the disastrous effect of the blizzard on our troops:*

'Two things have happened to interrupt the monotony of the comparative uneventfulness at the Dardanelles. One was that extraordinary blizzard of rain and bitter cold and snow in the last days of November. The other is the increase in the quality and quantity of the enemy's artillery fire, which is the first-fruits of the opening of the supply route from Germany to Turkey down the Danube to Rustchuk, thence by train through Adrianople to Urzun Kupru, and from there by road into the Gallipoli Peninsula.

'As to the blizzard, it is certain that the Turks suffered more than our men — dead bodies of those who had been drowned by the sudden spate of water down the gullies were washed right into our lines. On the other hand the increase in the Turks' artillery has raised the amount of damage his guns inflict only slightly, and as yet in no proportion to the imposing dimensions of the weapons he is believed to be receiving.'

We had learnt of large quantities of supplies now reaching the Turks on the Peninsula from Germany by the road passing near the head of the Gulf of Xeros. It was decided to send a battleship to destroy the bridge crossing the Kavak River.

THURSDAY DECEMBER 2ND. Hands turned out at 3 a.m., furled quarterdeck awning and prepared for sea. At 4 a.m. we weighed and proceeded out of harbour, escorted by destroyers

Fury and *Comet*, who took station on either quarter, and we increased speed to 16 knots, shaping a course for the east of Imbros. I had the morning watch at the guns, my first gun watch. It was not light till we were well past the south of Imbros and then the destroyers took station on either bow. Kephalo abeam about 8 a.m. and we were steering just to the west of Suvla Point. Weather conditions excellent, beautiful clear day, not cold, with gentle northerly breeze. We saw in Kephalo: *Swiftsure*, *Bacchante*, *Edgar*, two large monitors, several small monitors and other small craft. I also saw the small emergency harbour 'netted in', to the southward of Kephalo in the sandy bay. We gave Suvla Point a wide berth, but could plainly see some merchantmen and monitors in the Bay. Rounding the point we started to zigzag, only a few degrees either side of our course, and gave Arapos Bay a wide berth as they now have a couple of big howitzers there. On the bridge they thought they sighted a submarine's periscope on the starb. hand, but the destroyer could not find anything. When Cape Xeros was abeam, or slightly before this, we sighted and signalled *Endymion*, who was very difficult to distinguish against the background. 10.30 a.m. 'Action' was sounded off, but we hear that the after turret is not to fire, only fore turret and P 1 at the bridge itself, while the 'nine-twos' were to look after batteries and be ready with a shrapnel for troops. At 11 a.m. *Endymion* and the monitor were well astern of us, Xeros Island abeam. Some 'small stuff' meant for us, but 100 yds short.

Eased down and at 11.05 stopped and got into position; laid out *Reindeer* mark buoy and opened fire with shrapnel, which was meant for a caravan convoy crossing the bridge as we arrived — but both rounds burst a long way short. At 11.12 fore turret opened fire on the bridge at 10,000 yds, and after half a dozen rounds (very interesting to watch through the after-turret range-finder) I saw one column of the bridge and two spans were demolished altogether.

They fired some shrapnel at us a long way short and then hit us on the side with a little 3-pdr proj. We turned right round at 11.40 and closed in to 8,000 yds, while they went on with piffling little stuff at us and at the monitor, which achieved nothing. We went on with 12-in. at the stone bridge and then shifted target occasionally along the road and fired at a wooden bridge further up. At 11.50, P 1 opened fire for a few rounds but, owing to the guns being worn, did very poor practice and was soon relieved by fore turret.

Between 12.15 and 12.25 we were hit half a dozen times, once on a deadlight forward, once dented side-plating, two on P 3 turret; and remainder on armour.

All this time it was most interesting to watch two mounted gentlemen near the bridge, also a wagon and some horses, all quite unperturbed by our bombardment. Our mission completed, we steamed back to Mudros, arriving at our anchorage at 8 p.m.

SATURDAY DECEMBER 4TH. As usual we had to send 50 men to *Olympic* to coal her all day and eventually had to go on all night. It is a beastly shame to use the men out of H.M. ships as navvies and still worse not to pay them a cent extra for it.

The officers of *Olympic* say that if the ship went to Naples, they could get in enough coal in 24 hours to take them across the Atlantic. To hoist in 1,000 tons here takes a week and the people in *Olympic* put every obstacle in our way.

Signal from Admiral: 'Our submarine (*E 11*) in the Sea of Marmara reports attack on Ismid Railway, slight damage. Also sinking of destroyer *Yar Hissar* by torpedo, 40 of crew and two officers were picked up and placed on board sailing ship; also sinking steamship *Bosphorus*.'

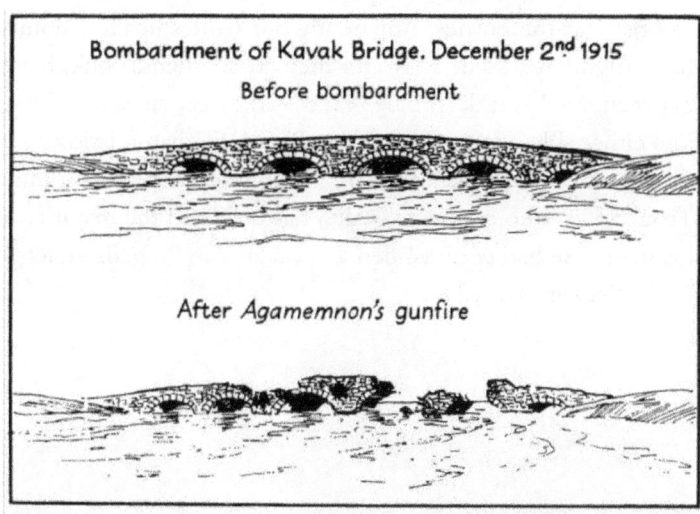

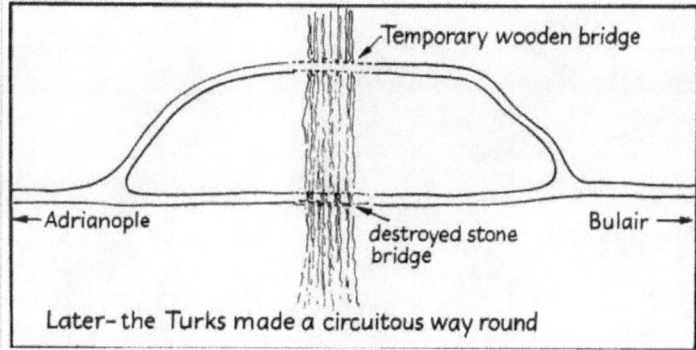

All the Turkist heavy weapons and ammunition had to be brought along this solitary road to Gallipoli passing over Kavak Bridge. Its destruction could only be brought about by naval gunfire from the Gulf of Xeres

SATURDAY DECEMBER 11TH. No news at all nowadays, at least what there is is too depressing to read. The Servians are absolutely smashed; our army in Servia is stated to be retreating (according to our Press) right back into Greece where the Greeks have stated they will protect them and not allow hostile troops over the border. Apparently our battleships at Salonika have frightened them a lot and they are in such a funk, being between devil and deep blue sea, that they get smashed if they join either side. Some more of the British Servian mission have turned up at Salonika, and are being sent here till Admiral Troubridge (who is now at Malta) has collected the majority of his men. (He had commanded a naval artillery brigade attached to the Servian Army.)

FIFTEEN: EVACUATION OF GALLIPOLI

SUNDAY DECEMBER 12TH. French battleships *République* and *Suffren* left at 8 a.m., destination unknown. That now leaves us with no French warships in these waters.

During the last few weeks troops have been brought back from Suvla every night and none sent back to replace them. Clearly the evacuation of Suvla and possibly Anzac is planned and Captain Godfrey has again gone to Anzac to get some guns away, not his old battery, but the heavy guns. Lieutenant Gardner is also going to Suvla, and we learn of small craft to be prepared.

Wahine, the Malta mail steamer, is not to carry any mail for Malta except the official one, on account of the important operations at Suvla. I think they are afraid of any news falling into enemy submarine's hand.

Signal from V. A. to S.N.O. Mudros: '*Chatham* is to leave Mudros so as to arrive at Kephalo at daylight tomorrow. *Agamemnon* is to be at short notice from daylight tomorrow until further orders.' Probably to engage *Goeben* should she break out.

Our Servian allies are reported to have retired right back into Greece, but the Bulgarians are said not to be crossing after them.

Chatham sailed during the 1st Watch. *Mars* and *Magnificent* arrived with no troops but with boats, etc., for Suvla evacuation.

TUESDAY DECEMBER 14TH. Dense fog came on at 4.30

a.m. and lasted till 10, when it turned quite fine with sunshine.

Just after noon both our picket-boats, together with two boats of the *Glory*, left in tow for Kephalo prior to the evacuation of Suvla. Paul has gone in the first boat with P.O. Barlow, and Anderson in No. 2 with Brooks, both boats fitted as before with Maxims. Meanwhile, we are getting off advance parties in armed boarding steamers, some of them arriving at Mudros early when the fog cleared — all troops from Anzac and Suvla. They told us how both beaches now get shelled every night with shrapnel, which makes things difficult as night is the only time work can be done.

6 p.m. Signal from steamer sending out S.O.S. near Cape Matapan. I suppose it is only another steamer getting strafed which is now a daily recurrence.

Transports *Alaunia* and *Ascania* sailed, full of troops recently brought off the Peninsula, destination unknown, possibly Salonika.

Lieutenant Dawson and 20 marines landed to take charge of the mutinous Greek crew of *Osmanieh* who have emulated their friends in *Aragon*. They were marched up to the camp on Ispatho Island and turned over to the military authorities.

Signal from principal Naval Transport Officer to Admiral: 'There are 7,000 troops to be embarked on last night of intermediate stage of operations Dec. 17th. All ships, which would be employed, are required for final operations 18th and 19th, which would entail heavy strain on personnel. May I use *Sentinel, Skirmisher, Prince Edward* and *Queen Victoria* for work on 17th? This would ease situation, but they should not arrive Imbros till daylight 19th.'

SATURDAY DECEMBER 18TH. At one hour's notice so could not go ashore again.

Signal from Admiral to all ships: 'No signals are to be transmitted by W/T unless absolutely necessary on anything but short distance. All signals from Mudros to Kephalo are to be made by the cable.'

This ought to improve my Middle Watch in the decoding office!

There is to be only one hospital-ship off Suvla and Anzac tomorrow — the final night of operations — as they were delayed one day, owing to bad weather. Seven thousand troops are to come off tonight. The General in charge at Suvla is to be accommodated in *Heliotrope* with staff. *Doris* arrived in the afternoon from Malta and left shortly afterwards probably for Suvla.

Several large empty transports arrived from Salonika, presumably to take the Suvla and Anzac troops down to Alexandria shortly after the evacuation. *Tunisian* and *Ulysses* were amongst them.

Heard that a merchantman *Tintoretto*, while on her way up from Malta, sighted two submarines with their parent ship. Merchantman opened fire, sank one submarine, damaged the other and sank the supply ship. We hear many such reports, some being exaggerations.

A few days ago a patrol boat captured a Greek caique with a chart, which had red crosses plotted in different positions along coastlines. This, we presume to be enemy supply bases for submarines, but it may have been done as a ruse, so that our submarine-hunters will lose time over the ubiquitous foe.

On her way home last time *Mauretania* put in to Naples to coal and the British Admiralty invited a commission of American, Dutch and Swedish officials to inspect her for war material. This was on account of the German allegations about our improper usage of hospital-ships. This may or may not be true, but I hope not true; anyhow this commission obviously proved the charge to be a falsehood.

I think this confusion arose over the fact that we were always changing over transports to hospital ships — see list below.

By the time notification of these changes reached the German Navy adverse reports of the ships' former activities were still coming in.

A few hospital ships out here of late. A contrast to only two ships with which we started the campaign in February.

Soudan
Valdivia
Dunvegan Castle
Somali
Aberdonian
Guildford Castle
Rewa
Assay
Grantully Castle
Plussey
Neuralia
Letitia
Cawdor Castle
Seang Choon
Kinfauns Castle
Gloster Castle
Cecile
Britannic
Kildonan Castle
Sicilia
Egypt
Glenart Castle

Clan MacGillivray (since converted)
Dover Castle
Dunluce Castle
Devanha
Kara Para
Dongola
Aquitania
Landfranc
Mauretania
Delta
Salta

Hospital-yachts
Liberty
Sunbeam(Lord Brassey)
Eileen (Joel)

SUNDAY DECEMBER 19TH. At 3 a.m. many boarding steamers, including *Abbasieh* and *Osmanieh*, arrived with the 7,000 troops from Suvla and Anzac. These were placed on board all other battleships except us, as we are at short notice probably in order to fight *Goeben* if she breaks out.

How I wish I could be helping at Gallipoli again; it is awful having to remain static in this place.

They say we have left only 16,000 troops at Suvla and Anzac altogether, who are coming off tonight with the exception of wounded and R.A.M.C. people, who may have to be left behind. The remaining guns will be blown up and the rest of the stores destroyed by gunfire in the morning. The destroyers and monitors will be taking an active part and are provided with extra shrapnel for use against the Turks who may molest the withdrawal.

Another beautiful night for the evacuation, flat calm and a nice bright moon, certainly an ideal night.

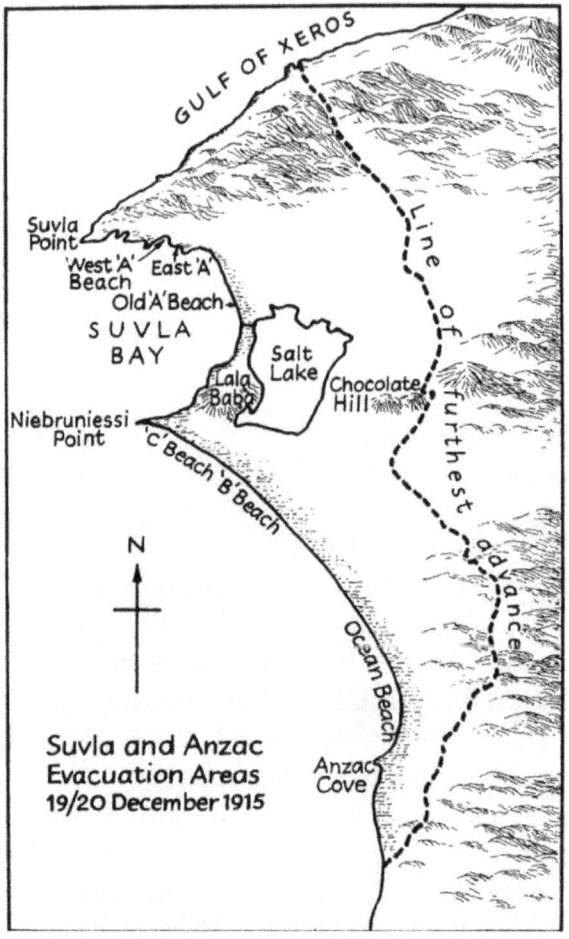

Sulva and Anzac evacuation area. December 19th/20th 1915. Since landing at Sulva four months earlier our troops had joined up with Anzac, but failed to make much progress inland

MONDAY DECEMBER 20TH. At 2.45 a.m. the ancient

battleship *Mars* arrived, filled with Australians and New Zealand troops.

We heard early by W/T that the evacuation of Suvla and Anzac had been carried out with wonderful success, there being no casualties at Anzac and only two killed and three wounded at Suvla. W/T signal at 6.59 a.m. from Gen. Birdwood to General Bing: 'Your 0500. Many thanks, your whole arrangements have worked out magnificently and I heartily congratulate all.'

We certainly had Providence with us this time; for we were prepared for enormous casualties, Kephalo being full of hospital-ships, also this place and all the stationary hospitals are cleared for the fresh cases.

At 7.10 a.m. all our blister ships and monitors opened fire and shelled the whole of the beach and 'searched' for Turks.

At 7.30 a.m. all the armed boarding-steamers started arriving full with troops: *Heroic, Hazel, Snaefell, Reindeer, Rowan*, etc., also *Abbasieh, El Kahira, Osmanieh*, etc.

At 3 p.m. *Colne* and *Ribble* arrived with naval beach parties and later Mr Gardner returned, also three R.N.R. lieutenants from the beaches and our two picket-boats in tow of tug *Houghli*.

Regarding the evacuation of Suvla and Anzac, our beach party told us that altogether some 70,000 troops in addition to all guns (heavy, light and machine), all ammunition, a tremendous quantity of stores, all mules and other gear of various descriptions, have been got away from Suvla and Anzac with quite immaterial casualties.

During the intermediate stage of operations (evening of the 18th) 10,000 troops were brought from Anzac and many men from Suvla, without a single casualty. Motor-lighters were used, of course, as well as the paddle-steamers, which could run in alongside the big piers at either of the beaches.

Before the intermediate stage, great preparations had previously been made by the beach-parties, to remove all valuable stores from the beaches which were not visible to the Turks. However, a great many of the stores had to be left behind, e.g., clothing, uniforms, food, big marquees, etc., but a large quantity of petrol was ready for pouring over these stores and igniting after the troops were off. Thus, absolutely everything that could be got off without being seen by the enemy was got off, even empty cartridge cylinders.

TUESDAY DECEMBER 21ST. Came on to blow hard from the south last night, so we stood by to let go second anchor. Aren't we lucky, for a day later might have spoilt the success of the whole evacuation. A great movement of transports today; four sailed in the evening: *Megantic*, a P. & O., *Ascania* and a Blue Funnel, all empty. During the afternoon *Chatham, Lord Nelson, Bacchante, Doris* and *Sir Thomas Picton* arrived all from Kephalo. *Magnificent*, which brought back our cutters, sailed later with *Saturnia, Knight Templar*, etc.

During the Last Dog a ship was sending up signals of distress in the outer anchorage. After we had sent boats to assist, it was found that *Abbasieh* had rammed a ship in the outer anchorage, but there was no underwater damage.

All destroyers put to sea at 9 p.m. to look for motor-lighters which broke adrift in the gale while coming round from Kephalo.

WEDNESDAY DECEMBER 22ND. Admiral DeRobeck arrived at 2.30 p.m. in the yacht *Eileen* (Joel) and hoisted his flag in *Lord Nelson*. R.A. Wemyss shifted his flag to *Europa*, while R.A. Christian shifted flag to *Swiftsure*. R.A. Wemyss is going to take over C.-in-C. East Indies. General Sir Charles Munro is going home to take command of the 1st Army Corps in succession to Sir Douglas Haig.

Signal from Admiral: 'The Admiralty has sent me the following message: "Judging from results, the evacuation reflects credit on the organisation and work of the Navy and the Admiralty wish to convey their appreciation to you and all officers and men." I heartily congratulate all officers and men.'

SATURDAY DECEMBER 25TH. Once again Christmas Day, and one of the merriest ones in spite of conditions. I had the forenoon watch and First Dog but ran picket-boat a good part of the time. We received on board for church among others Comdr Nasmith, V.C. (*E 11*), Comdr Boyle, V.C. (*E 14*), Comdr Brodie, D.S.O. On account of picket-boat duty I was the only midshipman not at church and came off rather the worse for cocktails. Before I got back to the ship, a Taube dropped three bombs aimed at us from a pretty good height, which fell about 50 yds clear and all burst properly; she then dropped some bombs close to *Aragon*, where the Admiral, R.A. Wemyss, Munro, etc., were on the promenade deck. Aeroplane was not fired at.

We made merry with the wardroom in the evening while myself and four others manned the steam-launch and took back Walker and Berthon to their destroyers. It ended in our not getting back from the *Racoon* till midnight.

Hospital ship *Britannic* arrived at 4 p.m., this is her first trip out here; she has not long been completed.

MONDAY DECEMBER 27TH. A day for bombardment.

We shortened in, weighed and shaped a course for Gaba Tepe at knots escorted by *Scorpion*, *Arno* and *Lydiard*. At 4 p.m. we were off Kum Tepe and sounded off 'Action'; the aeroplane had left Kephalo and was ready to spot for us. About 4.15 or slightly after the mark buoy was dropped and the ship being still, the fore turret opened fire at 12,000 yds on a camp over the hill at Suan Dere. No aeroplane correction for a few minutes and finally after a long delay another round was fired. Then the after turret carried on single rounds alternately with the fore turret, aeroplane spotting for each shot, until about 15 rounds from both turrets had been fired. Then a Taube came up and, being much higher, unsuccessfully attacked our aeroplane, which was quite amusing to watch. Our machine was also under heavy fire all the time and had one of her wire stays shot away and so had to return. We then fired two salvoes with the whole broadside and steamed back to Kephalo, coming to anchor again at 6 p.m. Fluter then went to make his report to the Rear-Admiral, for apparently the aeroplane man was a fool and made us waste a costly 20 12-in. full charge and 10 9.2-in., to the best of our knowledge without doing any damage.

The two big monitors were also bombarding.

TUESDAY DECEMBER 28TH. Weighed at 3.45 a.m. and proceeded out to Kephalo, shaping a course for Port Mudros, where we came to anchor in our usual billet at 8 a.m.

We now realised that Cape Helles area is to be evacuated, thus ending the whole Dardanelles campaign. The next few days of my diary concern Agamemnon's minor part in this well-planned evolution.

SATURDAY JANUARY 1ST 1916. New Year's Day and quite an amusing one for me. Lieutenant Crookshank was appointed to Helles as beach officer. We all felt such an urge to take part in the Evacuation that Pearson decided to break out of the ship and go with him, as assistant. We made arrangements about watches to avoid Pearson's disappearance from being discovered. At 9 a.m. I hid Pearson in the picket-boat and took him with Crookshank to *Barry*, which was sailing at noon for Gallipoli. However, our first misfortune was Fluter's court of inquiry over our wine bills; after he had been honoured with 10 minutes of my company, the old devil wanted Pearson, and so a general hunt ensued. Since he had to be produced, somehow, it ended in my confiding in the officer of the watch the whole yarn about his breakout. The O.O.W. kindly provided a boat for a phoney duty trip and I convinced Pearson that he couldn't possibly get away, and I brought him back. But meanwhile, The Rabbit had found out somehow and sounded me for information, so in the end we told him the whole yarn, which he took very sportingly, and we both had to give our paroles never to break out again.

SUNDAY JANUARY 2ND. *Empress of Britain* arrived and filled up with Australian troops for Alexandria. The Royal Engineers on the beach here have started to pack up a lot of their gear to be sent home together with a lot of stuff already arrived from Helles.

MONDAY JANUARY 3RD. Picket-boat, having been equipped and rigged for the coming operations at Helles, left with MacLeish at 7.30 a.m. The Admiralty and Fluter having gone mad, we started a new instruction course on account of our exam for acting sub. coming off in September. We are furious. About 1.15 p.m., I looked out of the scuttle to see a big steamer coming towards us and wasted no time getting up on deck expecting to get knocked flat when she hit us. Suddenly a crashing noise aft which I at once realised was only Fluter's sternwalk getting a bad time. On deck it was a great joke for all except Fluter who came up looking perturbed. It appeared that S.S. *Simla*, trying to turn round was caught by the high wind, and could not avoid hitting our stern.

TUESDAY JANUARY 4TH. About two whole divisions have now been brought off from Helles by these Khedival steamers: *Osmanieh, Abbasieh, Prince Albar, El Kahira*, which have to be filled with coal as soon as they arrive, so we have a party frequently away all night. The armed boarding steamers *Redbreast, Redpole*, etc., are kept full up by the Egyptians. Several transports left today with troops for Alexandria.

Those d—d submarines have now sunk just about 90 of our merchantmen in the Mediterranean since they first came out here in June. The P. & O. *Geelong* is the latest casualty. Received memo no. 196 from Fluter prohibiting any wine bill until the 14th inst.

WEDNESDAY JANUARY 5TH. Signal that *E 2* has returned from Dardanelles having been in Sea of Marmara 24 days. She sank one steamer and damaged another; also destroyed 19 sailing vessels and shelled Mudania Railway Station. Both our cutters have left for the old *Mars* for transport to Helles. This morning each battleship sent over 10 tins of 16¼-lb charge to Helles for the final demolition purposes.

THURSDAY JANUARY 6TH. *Caledonia* left at 8 a.m. with troops presumably for Alexandria. Transports now leave daily.

FRIDAY JANUARY 7TH. Landed at 11 a.m. and enjoyed an energetic day walking with Anderson through Kondia to Castro, charging over hills and rough country exploring the island.

SATURDAY JANUARY 8TH. Calm and misty with much transport activity to and from Gallipoli via Kephalo. Reported from Gallipoli that between 4 a.m. and 8 a.m. over 100 shells were fired on all beaches more especially 'V' and 'W' Beaches. Signal to stand by for fresh attack on trenches. The Turks evidently realise our intentions this time; they go on shelling beaches incessantly and cause a lot of casualties. The final evacuation is coming off tonight in spite of the fact the wind has been blowing from the south the last two days and is still blowing a strong breeze. Silence is ordered on W/T high-power messages during the night, so as not to interfere with the shore transmission at the G.H.Q. and Kephalo. There are 12 hospital-ships in here, so we are taking all precautions once more.

SUNDAY JANUARY 9TH. Heard the wonderful news at 6 a.m. that the evacuation had been completed with great success. 'If we can't land, we *can* evacuate,' shouted the evacuated troops.

In the early morning *Abbasieh, Osmanieh, Princess Ena* arrived full of troops, and at 8 a.m. *Prince George* arrived with quite 2,500 men. Later, came three destroyers — *Lydiard, Laforey and Bulldog* — with nearly 1,000 men each. *Bulldog* came round during the forenoon and absolutely soused the wretched soldiers. Weather bright, but blowing a strong breeze from the south all day, as it has been for last 24 hours.

Crookshank, Torps and the 'wild man' (our Dr Spalding) returned from 'W' Beach in *Princess Ena* and *Bulldog*, and at 5 p.m. *Chatham* arrived with Generals and the naval beach-parties.

When the 24 motor-lighters left Kephalo in tow of tugs they soon found themselves facing a gale, causing practically all to break adrift with the crews still in them and later only five were found. This appears to have been almost our only loss in the whole operation.

Our beach-party told us this story of the Helles evacuation:

Owing to insufficient time and risk of betraying our intentions, it was not possible to make many preparations for the removal of much ammunition, stores, etc. Owing to the weather forecast, it was decided that the evacuation should be carried out earlier than at first anticipated, which necessitated leaving behind many million pounds' worth of stores and equipment.

Judging by messages they dropped into our trenches, it seemed obvious to the Turks that we were evacuating some days before we actually did. All day and part of the night they carried on shelling beaches and the night of the 7th, being a very fine night, they shelled still harder and made an unsuccessful attack in which they succeeded only in leaving their trenches on one end of the line.

On the night of the 8th, there was a strong breeze blowing from the south making a big swell, even in the harbours. At 11 p.m. the *Triad* arrived off 'W' Beach and made the junction of the Helles-Kephalo cable. There were 20,000 men to be got off during the night and it was not till 1.30 a.m. that the first men left the back lines of trenches. Destroyers were used at 'V' Beach alongside *River Clyde*, where most of the troops were evacuated as well as at 'W'. Only 1,000 men were brought off from 'Y' Beach in motor-lighters to the old battleships and troop carriers stationed off 'W' Beach. At 'X' Beach and Morto Bay no troops were brought off, but picket-boats and cutters were there lying off to look for stragglers.

At 4 a.m. the evacuation of the troops was complete, but, owing to the weather, it was decided not to get any more guns, motors, etc., off. Sixteen guns were left behind with much ammunition in a small white house which the monitors hoped to hit later. Tremendous quantities of stores we were able to burn, while motor cars, lorries, carts, wagons, etc., were put on top of the cliff open to our shellfire.

WEDNESDAY JANUARY 19TH. The army and navy again achieved the impossible, and every man was carried back to Mudros. The Gallipoli campaign had ended.

Extract from the Daily Mail, January 20th 1916
FINAL WATCH AT SUVLA.
BY A NAVAL OFFICER.
THE GENERAL LAST TO GO.
MINE TRAPS FOR TURKS

A *naval officer describing our evacuation of Suvla, in Gallipoli, writes under date December* 20:

We have just finished a week which had all the elements of the most acute anxiety for those in the highest command on land and sea. The Operations have not caused so much stir as those at Salonica, but for all that they are unique in, history, and their success (if a retreat can be called a success) has been so complete that it has staggered even, the most optimistic.

A REFLECTION ON THE DARDANELLES CAMPAIGN

Many books have been written by historians, journalists and admirals. I can only sum up what my diary appears to reveal.

We started with the easy task of subduing the Outer Forts and then landing demolition parties to destroy the guns, with relatively little opposition and small loss of life.

The second phase of sweeping the mines within the Straits and destroying the defences as far as the Narrows was never achieved. The 6-knot trawlers were most unsuitable in the face of effective close gunfire and searchlights, especially when they should have been sweeping against a 2-knot current instead of with it as they appear to have done. Why had Admiralty not envisaged the need for fast paddle-steamers to be fitted out for sweeping? They had at least 10 knots speed (for example, two of them, *Lorna Doone* and *Balmoral* at Southampton were good for 15 knots)

The mobile guns on the Asian shore were certainly a problem and none of our battleships was able to subdue them. They were largely the cause of minesweeping being brought to a halt and the army having to be called upon to invade Gallipoli.

Despite their poor protection against plunging shells and inadequate flash doors, the old battleships were fortunate in having no serious calamities from shellfire. Only a year later at Jutland did we pay for our inefficient armour protection when three battlecruisers blew up, and nearly a fourth — *Lion*.

Our submarines so gallantly operating in the Marmara (with the loss of more than half their number) contributed a very great share in weakening the enemy by cutting their vulnerable supply routes.

Lastly, had we known at the time of the Navy's final attack on March 18th 1915 that most of the forts were almost out of ammunition, there was perhaps a good chance of the Navy having succeeded in forcing the Narrows, but only provided efficient minesweepers had been made available at the time. The 'Beagle'-class destroyers might well have served the purpose.

On Gallipoli today, 24 cemeteries now commemorate almost 24,000 Commonwealth dead. These cemeteries are sited close to where men fell in battle, the graves being headstones placed horizontally in groups sometimes bordered by grass and surrounded by perennials and rosemary. All are most perfectly maintained by the Commonwealth War Graves Commission and are both beautiful and moving to see. The 100 ft obelisk standing on the tip of the Peninsula is known as the Helles War Memorial.

Agamemnon's dead have a small burial place of their own at Port Mudros. It lies in a little corner by the entrance to the Eastern Cemetery:

The race is not to the swift, nor the battle to the strong
But time and chance happeneth to them all.

Eccles. 9:11

SIXTEEN: GOOD-BYE TO *AGGIE*

There followed a few dreary months in *Agamemnon*, mostly based at Salonika, for the Macedonian front had replaced Gallipoli and there was no longer a need for our supply base at Mudros.

Our Franco-British line stretched across northern Greece with the British defending the eastern flank along a chain of lakes north-east of Salonika to the sea at Stavros. There was no fighting. Unexpectedly there came a splendid opportunity to man a patrol launch on the frontier lake at the eastern end of our line at Macedonia. Again I was lucky and found myself at a lonely outpost on the south shore of Lake Beshik living in a dug-out beside an armed launch with the following command:

Boat's crew: 1 P.O. and 3 men

Machine-gunners: 3 men with a Maxim gun

Military guard: 2 N.C.O.s and 12 K.R.R. men

Royal Artillery: 2 men and 2 horses and 1 Greek interpreter

We had to keep a watchful eye on 77 fishing boats and my duty was to count these boats when hauled ashore each evening and to patrol the lake each night. I lived alone in a very comfortable dug-out, often riding round the countryside sometimes calling on the mayors of local Greek villages, shooting duck with a 12-bore borrowed from Dick Wyndham. In the evening I was reading *The Riddle of the Sands* and Cowper's *Sailing Tours* by oil lamp. The fishermen (of Turkish origin) lived in little huts close by and sometimes invited me to coffee. Each week I would fetch the paymaster with pay for the troops at the east end of the lake guarding the Rendina Gorge by Stavros. They were the 60th Regt. and their standard of living in the Officers' Mess was proclaimed by the pile of empty cases outside the cookhouse, labelled 'Fortnum & Mason'. On the night of May 5th I was awakened by a distant glare in the sky and the next day I learnt that *Agamemnon* had shot down the Zeppelin *LZ 85*.

This sort of life was too good to last. After a few weeks I had to rejoin *Agamemnon* and we were soon ordered to Malta. To our disgust we were shortly facing exams for the rank of sub-lieutenant; the ordeal over we let go in celebrations with dinner parties ashore sometimes ending in *chorozzi* races. We would gently move the driver over, take the reins, and race furiously down the high street and sometimes into the sea *chorozzi* and all.

AFTERMATH

I was appointed to the coal-burning destroyer *Racoon*. On taking leave of Fluter he wrote some generous words on my flimsy. After all the unkind things written about him it was more than I deserved. I now found myself serving with an admirable captain, Kenneth Sworder, and Lyon Berthon as First Lieutenant. Amongst my other duties was that of navigator and we spent a whole year protecting convoys of transports all over the Mediterranean. It did not help matters when heavy weather would wash overboard the extra coal we had to carry on deck for some of the longer voyages. Only once did we lose a transport — *Cestrian* — with 1,000 horses on board, but we managed to save 1,000 soldiers. Though the French had different ideas on how best to protect a convoy, we worked in perfect harmony. Here are two examples:

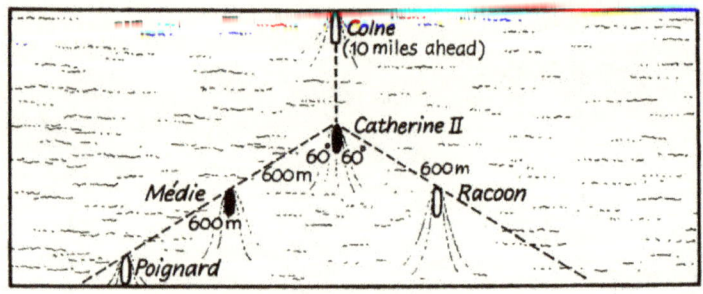

French 12-knot convoy June 17th 1917: two transports, *Catherine II* the more valuable, and *Médie*. Escort: French destroyer *Poignard* and British destroyers *Racoon* and *Colne*. Destination Salonika

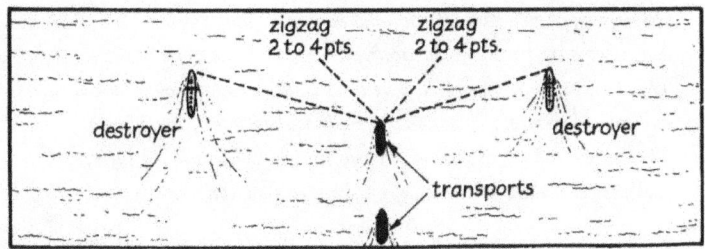

The British formation at same time

In both the French and British methods of escorting transports the convoy and escorts would alter course according to a prearranged plan a number of degrees from the path of advance. The escort would make small zigzags independently.

Only once did we visit the deserted Dardanelles to examine the entrance and here I excelled in my gunnery expertise, for my fourth round from the 4-in. gun brought down an approaching aircraft. Alas, it was the wrong bird: we fished an infuriated Admiral Usborne and his pilot from the sea — our own Senior Officer of the Dardanelles area on a reconnaissance. A last glimpse of the Dardanelles to savour for a lifetime.

The last year of war I spent in home waters in the oil-burning destroyer *Sylph*, part of Tyrwhitt's elite force based at Harwich for the costly struggle against German mines and torpedoes in the North Sea. There was quite enough excitement for me.

With the end of the war most of *Aggie*'s snotties gathered once more: their Lordships had decided to improve our minds at Cambridge University. Magdalene was one of the happiest years of my life. Very few of us felt we were scholars, yet a remarkable man, who had made such a deep impression during a few moments of meeting years before at Osborne, Rudyard Kipling, saw it like this:

Oh show me how a rose can shut and be a bud again!
Nay, watch my Lords of Admiralty, for they have the work in train.
They have taken the men that were careless lads at Dartmouth in 'Fourteen
and entered them in the landward schools as though no war had been.
They have piped the children of the seas from Falklands to the Bight,
and quartered them on the colleges to learn to read and write.

I was to spend the next twenty years at sea, but for some their lives had to change. The Government decided to slim down the Navy to a peacetime level, and about half of *Aggie*'s gunroom came under the Geddes axe. They had to seek a living elsewhere, some in Australia, some in New Zealand, and others in Kenya, until another war loomed up and brought them back to sea.

A NOTE TO THE READER

If you have enjoyed this book enough to leave a review on **Amazon** and **Goodreads**, then we would be truly grateful.

The Estate of H. M. Denham

Sapere Books is an exciting new publisher of brilliant fiction and popular history.

To find out more about our latest releases and our monthly bargain books visit our website: **saperebooks.com**

www.ingramcontent.com/pod-product-compliance
Lightning Source LLC
LaVergne TN
LVHW090039090426
835510LV00038B/677